CARNIVAL OF CONTAGION

Story by Bob Hall, with John West and Judy Diamond
Illustrated by Bob Hall
Colors by Nathaniel Hamel, John Kimmel, and Bob Hall
Lettering by Marie Kisling
"Master of Contagion" essay by Carl Zimmer
Production design by Aaron Sutherlen

Biology of HUMAN

Biology of Human is an alliance of science educators, artists, science writers, social scientists, and biomedical researchers working to increase public understanding about viruses and infectious disease.

For information see http://biologyofhuman.unl.edu.

SEPA SCIENCE EDUCATION PARTNERSHIP AWARD
Supported by the National Center for Research Resources, a part of the National Institutes of Health

UNIVERSITY OF NEBRASKA STATE MUSEUM

Nebraska UNIVERSITY OF Lincoln

UNIVERSITY OF NEBRASKA PRESS • LINCOLN & LONDON

Manufactured in the United States of America.

⊗

Library of Congress Cataloging-in-Publication Data
Names: Hall, Bob, 1944 October 16-author, illustrator. | West, John T., Jr.,
1967– author. | Diamond, Judy, author.
Title: Carnival of contagion / created and illustrated by Bob Hall ; with
John West and Judy Diamond ; "Master of Cantagion" essay by Carl Zimmer ;
colors by Nathaniel Hamel, John Kimmel, and Bob Hall ; lettering by Marie
Kisling ; Biology of Human.
Description: Lincoln : University of Nebraska Press, [2017] | Audience: Age
15–18. | Audience: Grade 9 to 12.
Identifiers: LCCN 2017022069 | ISBN 9781496205964 (pbk. : alk. paper)
Subjects: LCSH: Measles—Comic books, strips, etc. | Measles—Juvenile
literature. | Graphic novels.
Classification: LCC RA644.M5 H28 2017 | DDC 616.9/15—dc23 LC record available at
https://lccn.loc.gov/2017022069

Contents

CARNIVAL OF CONTAGION

Comic by Bob Hall
with John West & Judy Diamond

MASTER OF CONTAGION

Essay by Carl Zimmer

Meet the measles virus, one
of the most contagious viruses known.

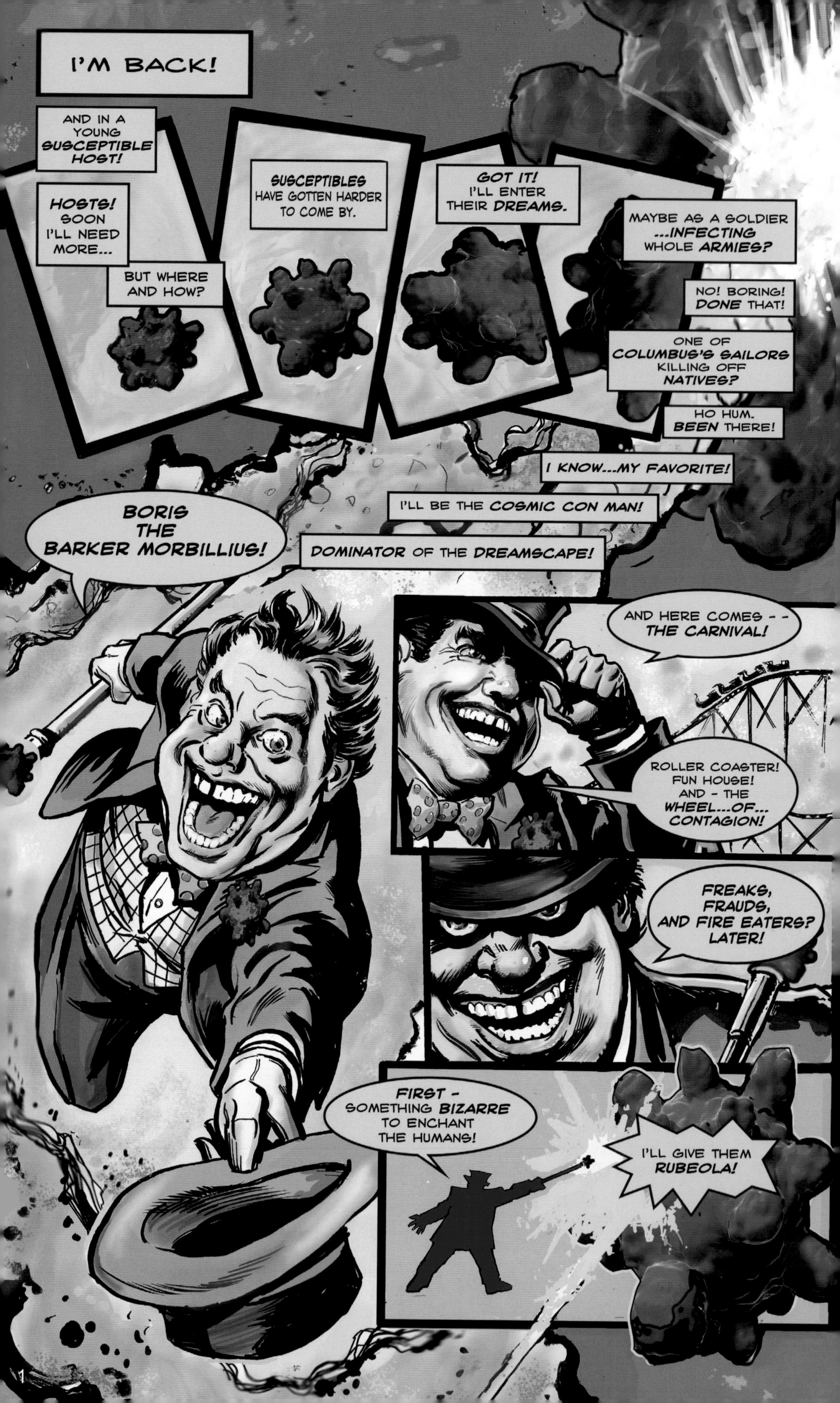

I'M BACK!
AND IN A YOUNG SUSCEPTIBLE HOST!
HOSTS! SOON I'LL NEED MORE...
BUT WHERE AND HOW?
SUSCEPTIBLES HAVE GOTTEN HARDER TO COME BY.
GOT IT! I'LL ENTER THEIR DREAMS.
MAYBE AS A SOLDIER ...INFECTING WHOLE ARMIES?
NO! BORING! DONE THAT!
ONE OF COLUMBUS'S SAILORS KILLING OFF NATIVES?
HO HUM. BEEN THERE!
I KNOW...MY FAVORITE!
I'LL BE THE COSMIC CON MAN!
BORIS THE BARKER MORBILLIUS!
DOMINATOR OF THE DREAMSCAPE!
AND HERE COMES - - THE CARNIVAL!
ROLLER COASTER! FUN HOUSE! AND - THE WHEEL...OF... CONTAGION!
FREAKS, FRAUDS, AND FIRE EATERS? LATER!
FIRST - SOMETHING BIZARRE TO ENCHANT THE HUMANS!
I'LL GIVE THEM RUBEOLA!

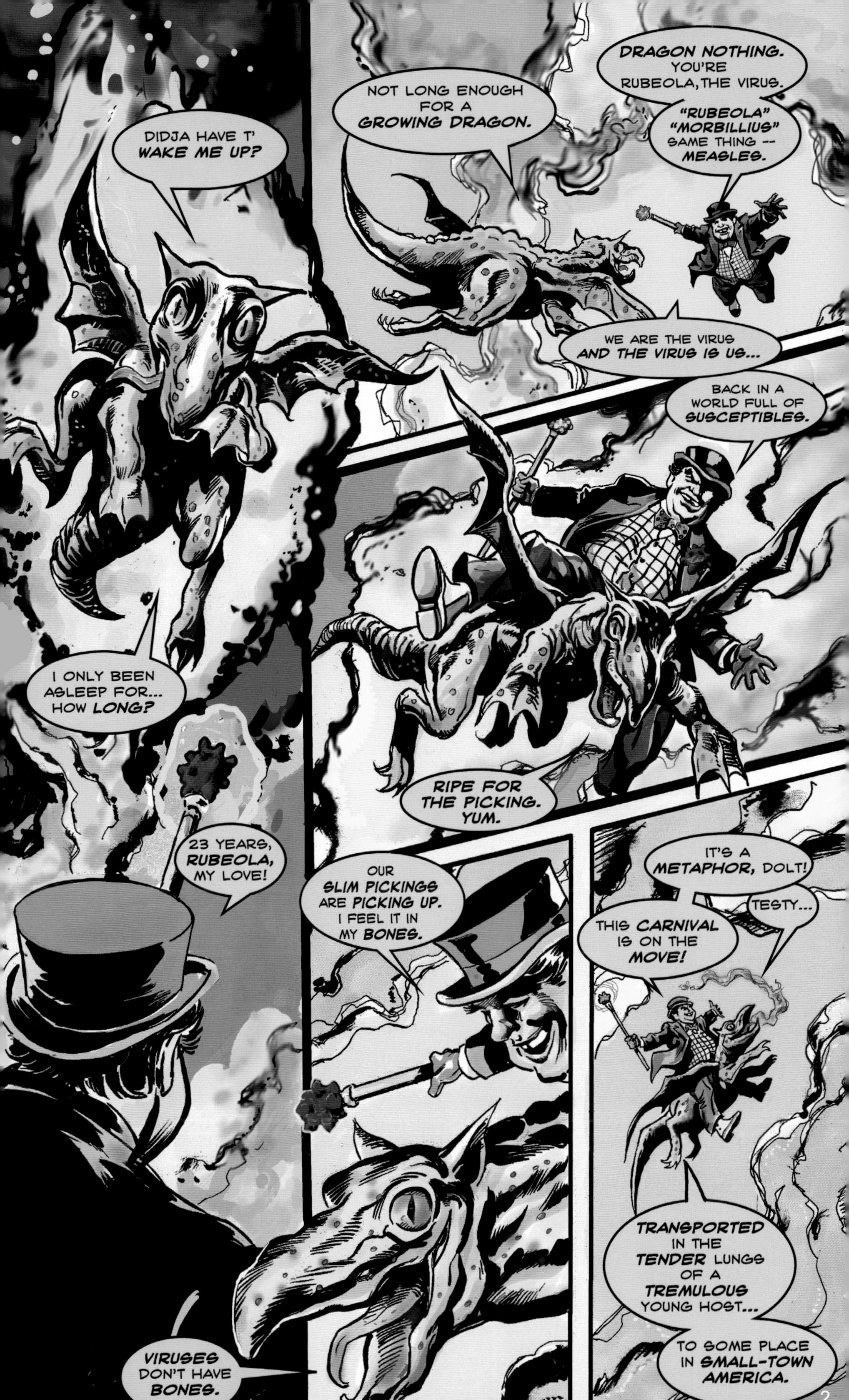
DIDJA HAVE T' WAKE ME UP?
I ONLY BEEN ASLEEP FOR... HOW LONG?
23 YEARS, RUBEOLA, MY LOVE!
VIRUSES DON'T HAVE BONES.
NOT LONG ENOUGH FOR A GROWING DRAGON.
DRAGON NOTHING. YOU'RE RUBEOLA, THE VIRUS.
"RUBEOLA" "MORBILLIUS" SAME THING -- MEASLES.
WE ARE THE VIRUS AND THE VIRUS IS US...
BACK IN A WORLD FULL OF SUSCEPTIBLES.
RIPE FOR THE PICKING. YUM.
OUR SLIM PICKINGS ARE PICKING UP. I FEEL IT IN MY BONES.
IT'S A METAPHOR, DOLT!
TESTY...
THIS CARNIVAL IS ON THE MOVE!
TRANSPORTED IN THE TENDER LUNGS OF A TREMULOUS YOUNG HOST...
TO SOME PLACE IN SMALL-TOWN AMERICA.

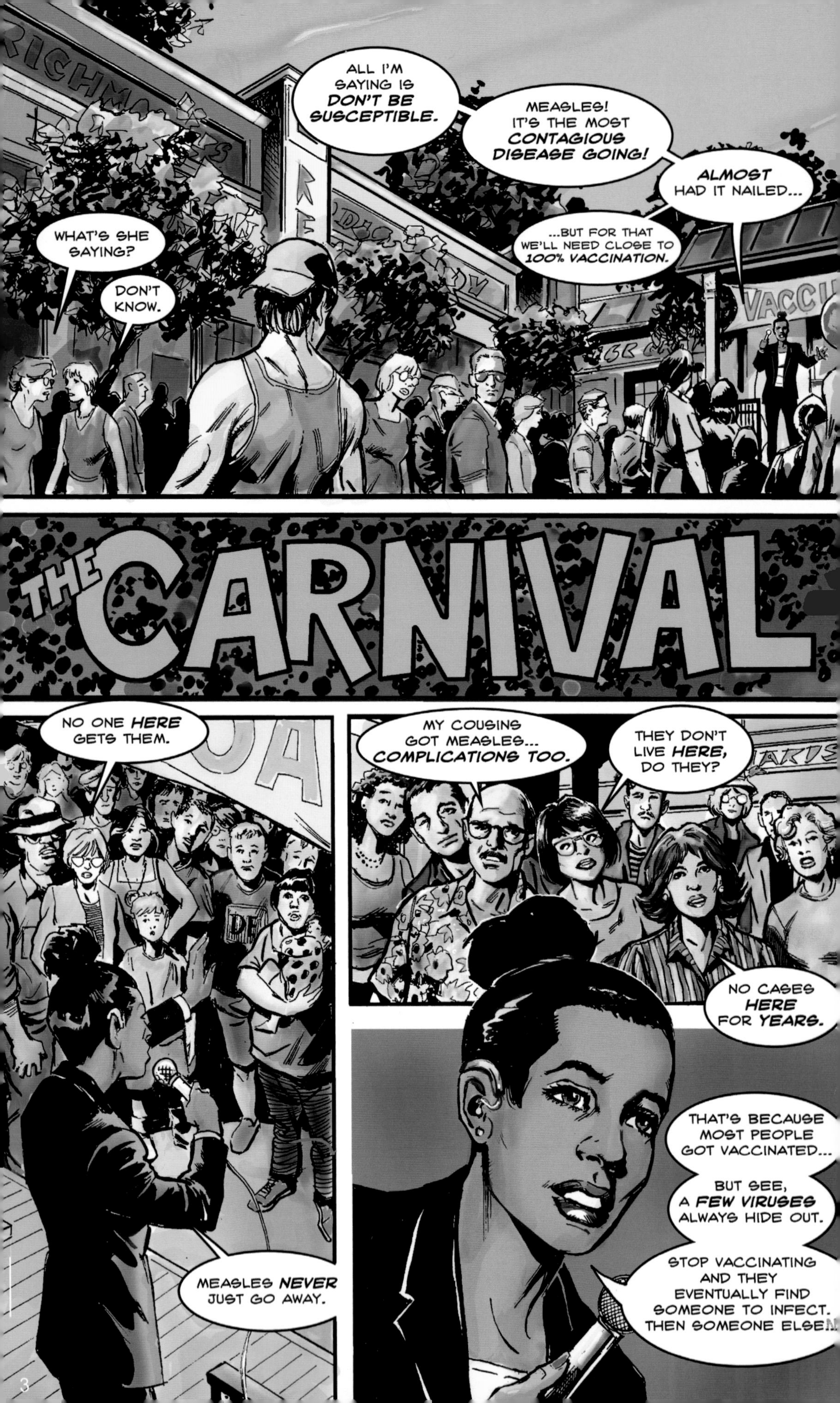
RICHMA
ALL I'M SAYING IS DON'T BE SUSCEPTIBLE.
MEASLES! IT'S THE MOST CONTAGIOUS DISEASE GOING!
ALMOST HAD IT NAILED...
...BUT FOR THAT WE'LL NEED CLOSE TO 100% VACCINATION.
WHAT'S SHE SAYING?
DON'T KNOW.
THE CARNIVAL
NO ONE HERE GETS THEM.
MEASLES NEVER JUST GO AWAY.
MY COUSINS GOT MEASLES... COMPLICATIONS TOO.
THEY DON'T LIVE HERE, DO THEY?
NO CASES HERE FOR YEARS.
THAT'S BECAUSE MOST PEOPLE GOT VACCINATED...
BUT SEE, A FEW VIRUSES ALWAYS HIDE OUT.
STOP VACCINATING AND THEY EVENTUALLY FIND SOMEONE TO INFECT. THEN SOMEONE ELSE...

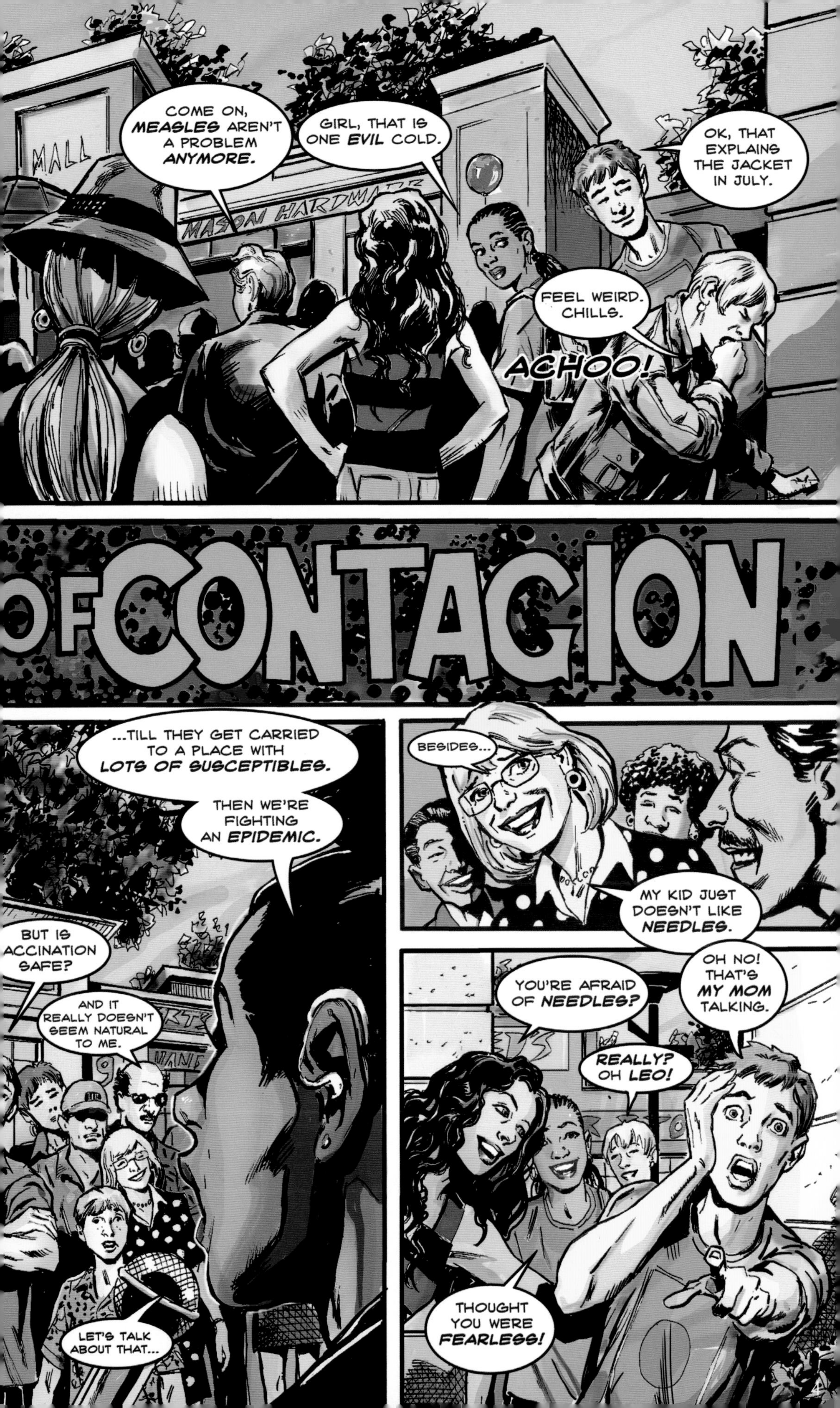
MALL
MASON HARDWARE
COME ON, MEASLES AREN'T A PROBLEM ANYMORE.
GIRL, THAT IS ONE EVIL COLD.
OK, THAT EXPLAINS THE JACKET IN JULY.
FEEL WEIRD. CHILLS.
ACHOO!
OF CONTAGION
...TILL THEY GET CARRIED TO A PLACE WITH LOTS OF SUSCEPTIBLES.
THEN WE'RE FIGHTING AN EPIDEMIC.
BUT IS ACCINATION SAFE?
AND IT REALLY DOESN'T SEEM NATURAL TO ME.
LET'S TALK ABOUT THAT...
BESIDES...
MY KID JUST DOESN'T LIKE NEEDLES.
YOU'RE AFRAID OF NEEDLES?
OH NO! THAT'S MY MOM TALKING.
REALLY? OH LEO!
THOUGHT YOU WERE FEARLESS!

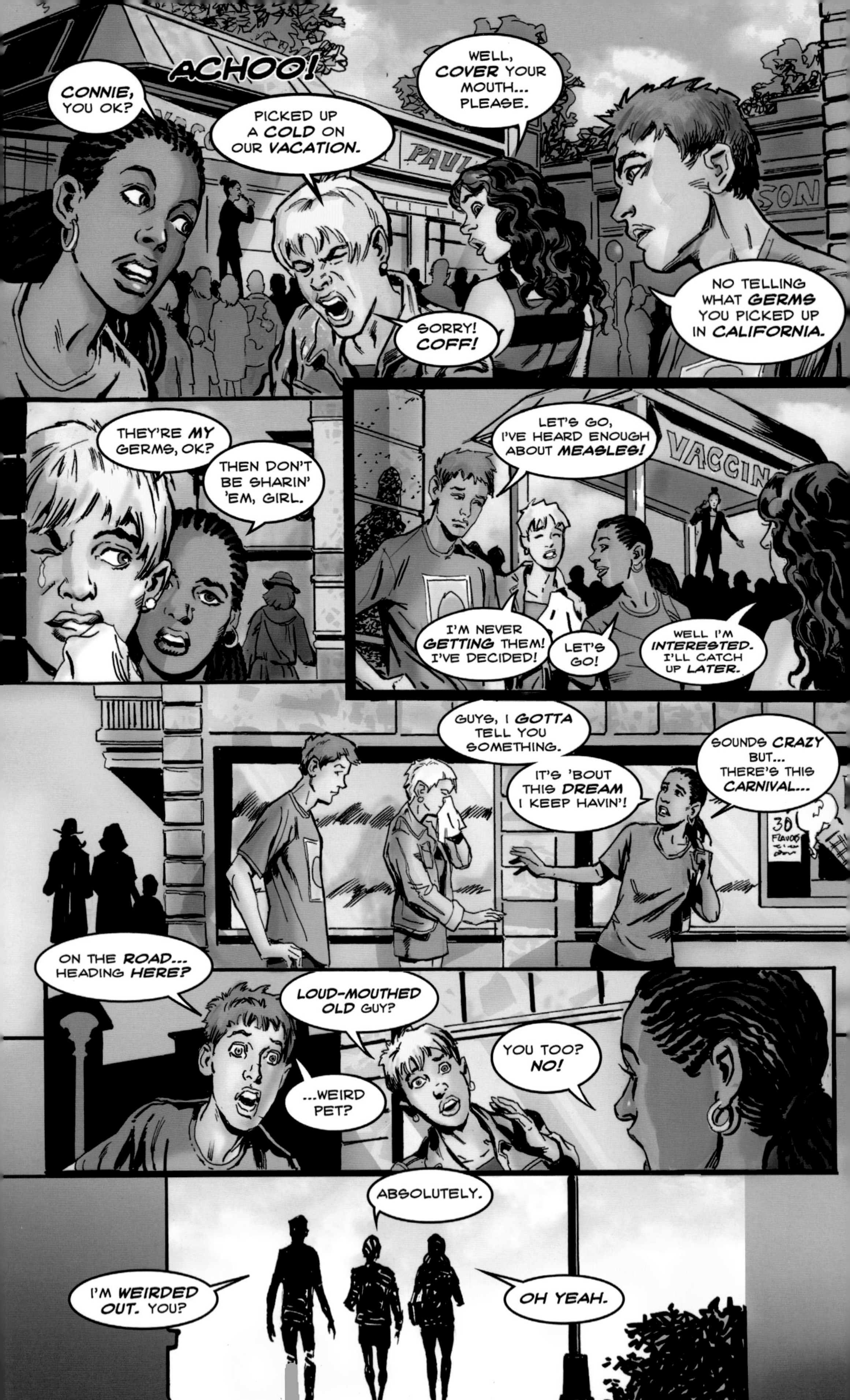
ACHOO!
CONNIE, YOU OK?
PICKED UP A COLD ON OUR VACATION.
WELL, COVER YOUR MOUTH... PLEASE.
SORRY! COFF!
NO TELLING WHAT GERMS YOU PICKED UP IN CALIFORNIA.
THEY'RE MY GERMS, OK?
THEN DON'T BE SHARIN' 'EM, GIRL.
LET'S GO, I'VE HEARD ENOUGH ABOUT MEASLES!
I'M NEVER GETTING THEM! I'VE DECIDED!
LET'S GO!
WELL I'M INTERESTED. I'LL CATCH UP LATER.
GUYS, I GOTTA TELL YOU SOMETHING.
IT'S 'BOUT THIS DREAM I KEEP HAVIN'!
SOUNDS CRAZY BUT... THERE'S THIS CARNIVAL...
ON THE ROAD... HEADING HERE?
LOUD-MOUTHED OLD GUY?
...WEIRD PET?
YOU TOO? NO!
ABSOLUTELY.
I'M WEIRDED OUT. YOU?
OH YEAH.

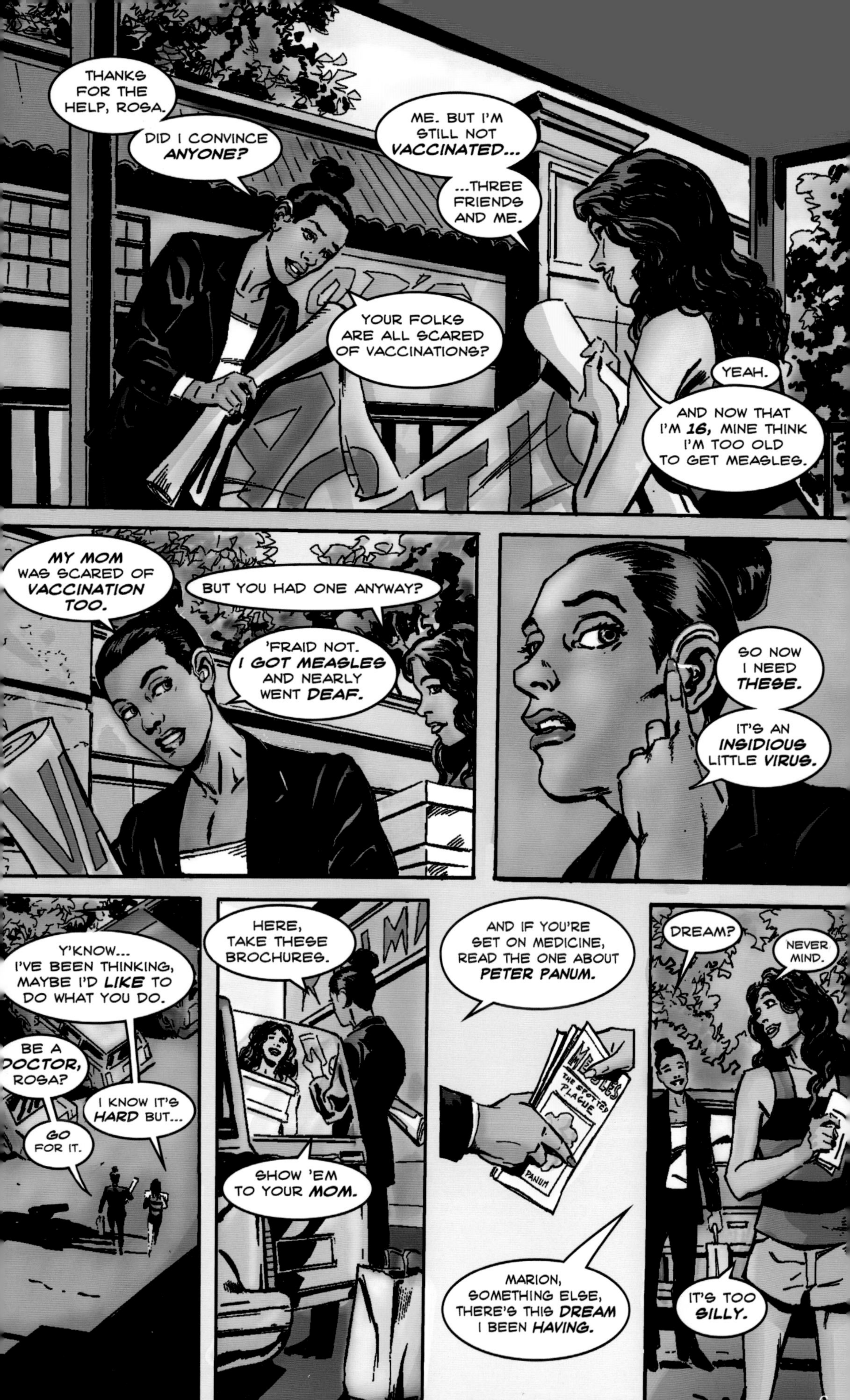
THANKS FOR THE HELP, ROSA.
DID I CONVINCE ANYONE?
ME. BUT I'M STILL NOT VACCINATED...
...THREE FRIENDS AND ME.
YOUR FOLKS ARE ALL SCARED OF VACCINATIONS?
YEAH.
AND NOW THAT I'M 16, MINE THINK I'M TOO OLD TO GET MEASLES.
MY MOM WAS SCARED OF VACCINATION TOO.
BUT YOU HAD ONE ANYWAY?
'FRAID NOT. I GOT MEASLES AND NEARLY WENT DEAF.
SO NOW I NEED THESE.
IT'S AN INSIDIOUS LITTLE VIRUS.
Y'KNOW... I'VE BEEN THINKING, MAYBE I'D LIKE TO DO WHAT YOU DO.
BE A DOCTOR, ROSA?
I KNOW IT'S HARD BUT...
GO FOR IT.
HERE, TAKE THESE BROCHURES.
SHOW 'EM TO YOUR MOM.
AND IF YOU'RE SET ON MEDICINE, READ THE ONE ABOUT PETER PANUM.
MEASLES
THE SPOTTED PLAGUE
PANUM
MARION, SOMETHING ELSE, THERE'S THIS DREAM I BEEN HAVING.
DREAM?
NEVER MIND.
IT'S TOO SILLY.

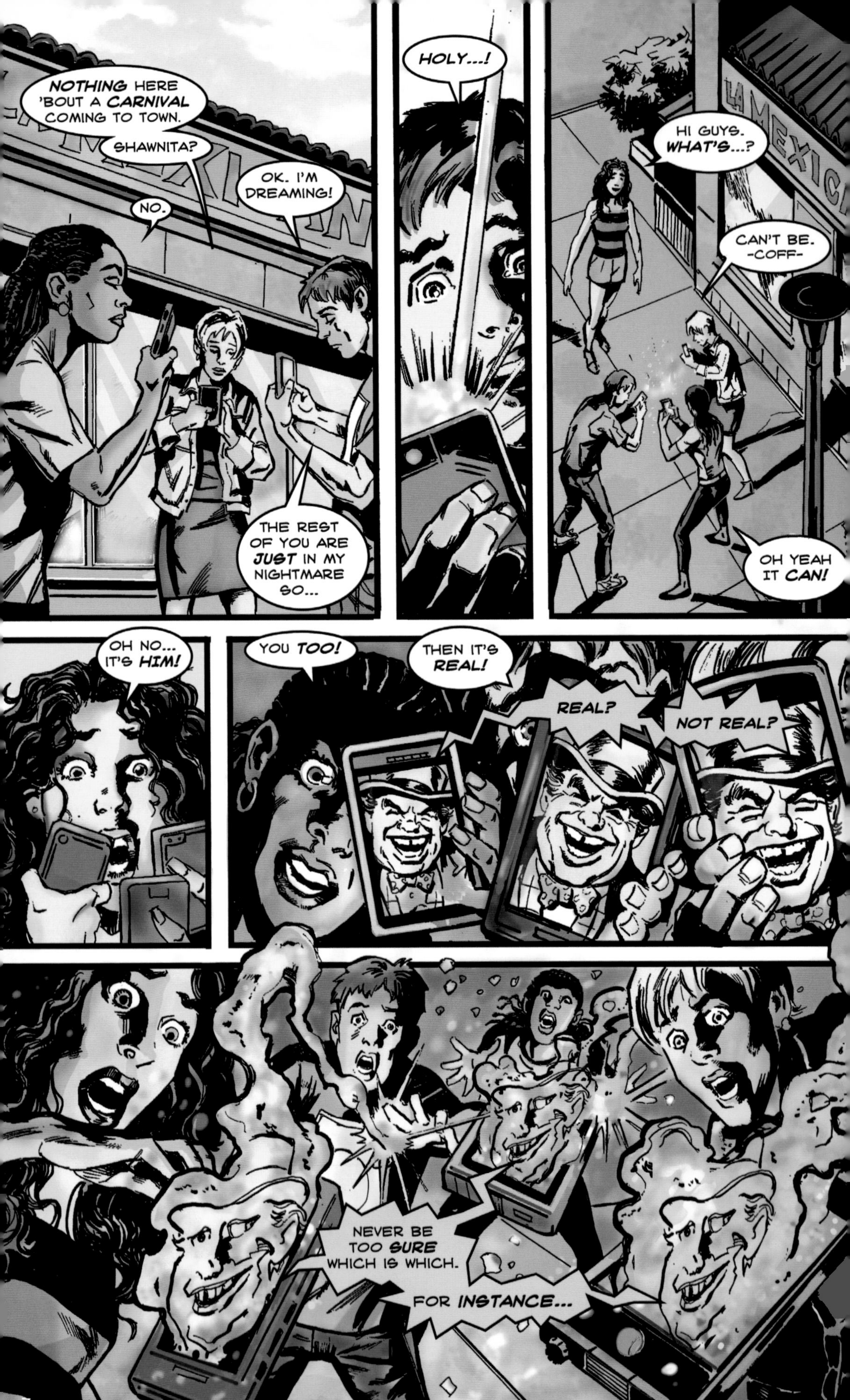
NOTHING HERE 'BOUT A CARNIVAL COMING TO TOWN.
SHAWNITA?
NO.
OK. I'M DREAMING!
THE REST OF YOU ARE JUST IN MY NIGHTMARE SO...
HOLY...!
HI GUYS. WHAT'S...?
CAN'T BE. -COFF-
OH YEAH IT CAN!
OH NO... IT'S HIM!
YOU TOO!
THEN IT'S REAL!
REAL?
NOT REAL?
NEVER BE TOO SURE WHICH IS WHICH.
FOR INSTANCE...

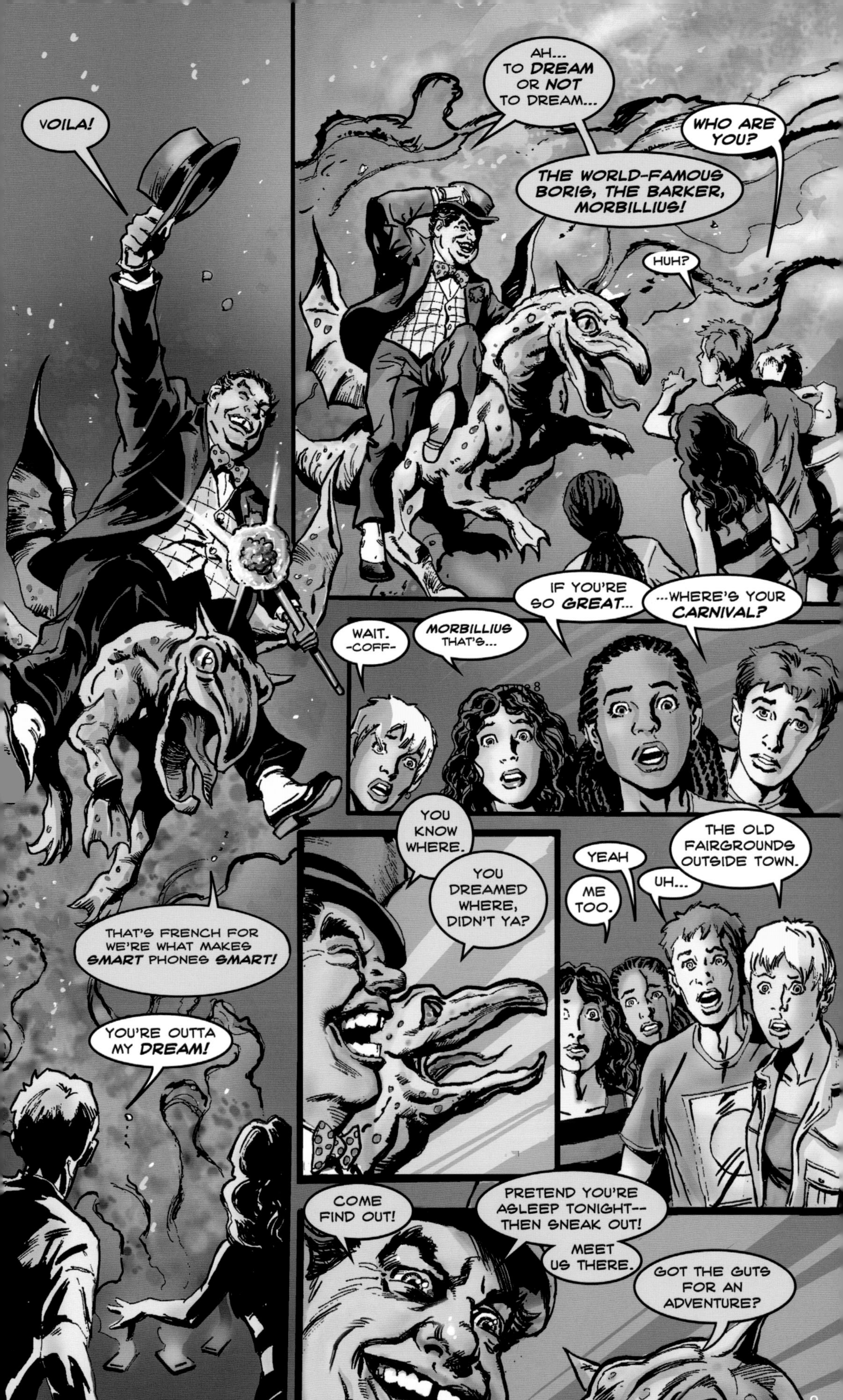

VOILA!
THAT'S FRENCH FOR WE'RE WHAT MAKES SMART PHONES SMART!
YOU'RE OUTTA MY DREAM!
AH... TO DREAM OR NOT TO DREAM...
WHO ARE YOU?
THE WORLD-FAMOUS BORIS, THE BARKER, MORBILLIUS!
HUH?
WAIT. -COFF-
MORBILLIUS THAT'S...
IF YOU'RE SO GREAT...
...WHERE'S YOUR CARNIVAL?
YOU KNOW WHERE.
YOU DREAMED WHERE, DIDN'T YA?
YEAH
ME TOO.
UH...
THE OLD FAIRGROUNDS OUTSIDE TOWN.
COME FIND OUT!
PRETEND YOU'RE ASLEEP TONIGHT-- THEN SNEAK OUT!
MEET US THERE.
GOT THE GUTS FOR AN ADVENTURE?

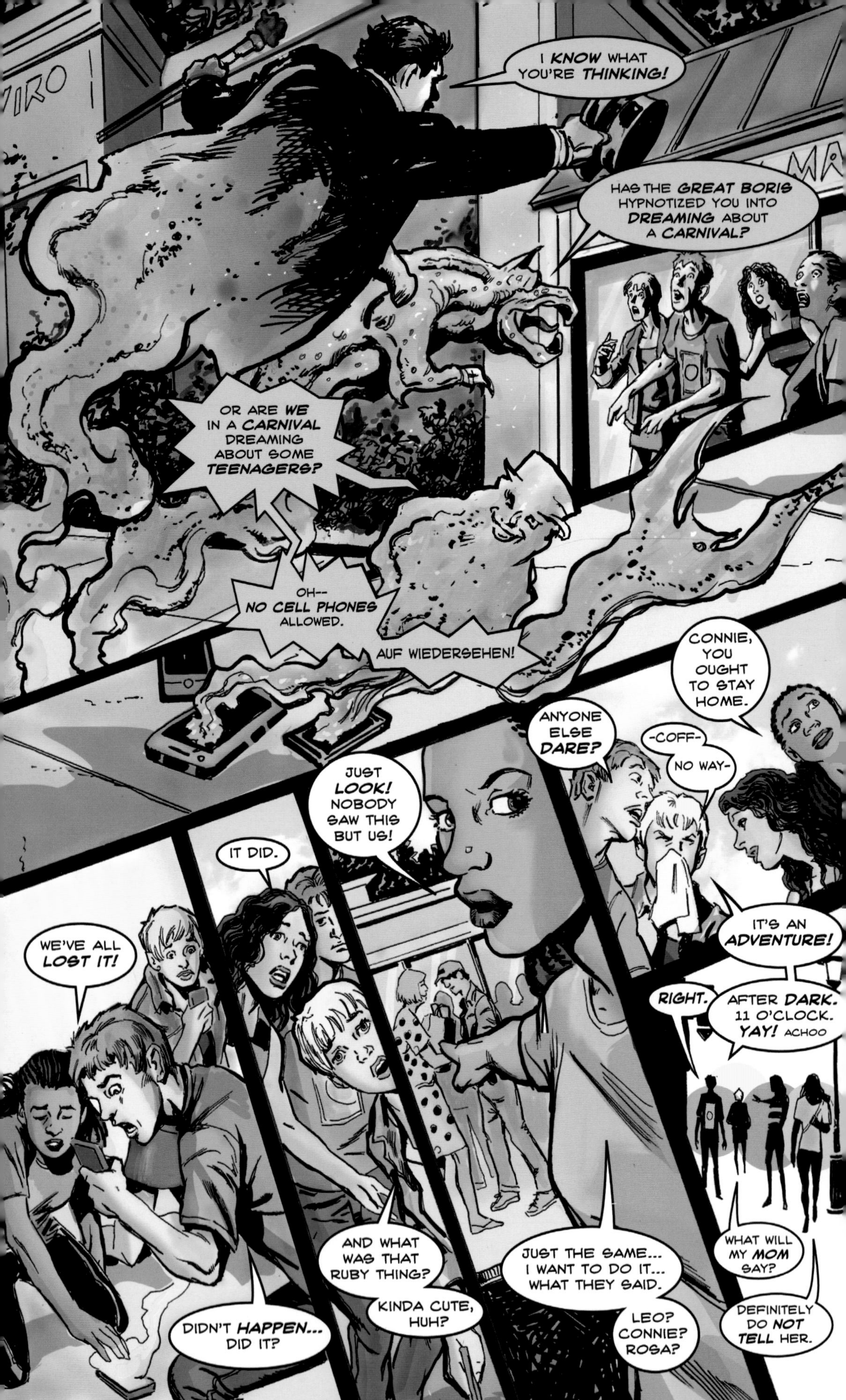
IRO
I KNOW WHAT YOU'RE THINKING!
HAS THE GREAT BORIS HYPNOTIZED YOU INTO DREAMING ABOUT A CARNIVAL?
OR ARE WE IN A CARNIVAL DREAMING ABOUT SOME TEENAGERS?
OH-- NO CELL PHONES ALLOWED.
AUF WIEDERSEHEN!
WE'VE ALL LOST IT!
DIDN'T HAPPEN... DID IT?
IT DID.
AND WHAT WAS THAT RUBY THING?
KINDA CUTE, HUH?
JUST LOOK! NOBODY SAW THIS BUT US!
JUST THE SAME... I WANT TO DO IT... WHAT THEY SAID.
LEO? CONNIE? ROSA?
ANYONE ELSE DARE?
-COFF-
NO WAY-
CONNIE, YOU OUGHT TO STAY HOME.
IT'S AN ADVENTURE!
RIGHT.
AFTER DARK. 11 O'CLOCK. YAY! ACHOO
WHAT WILL MY MOM SAY?
DEFINITELY DO NOT TELL HER.

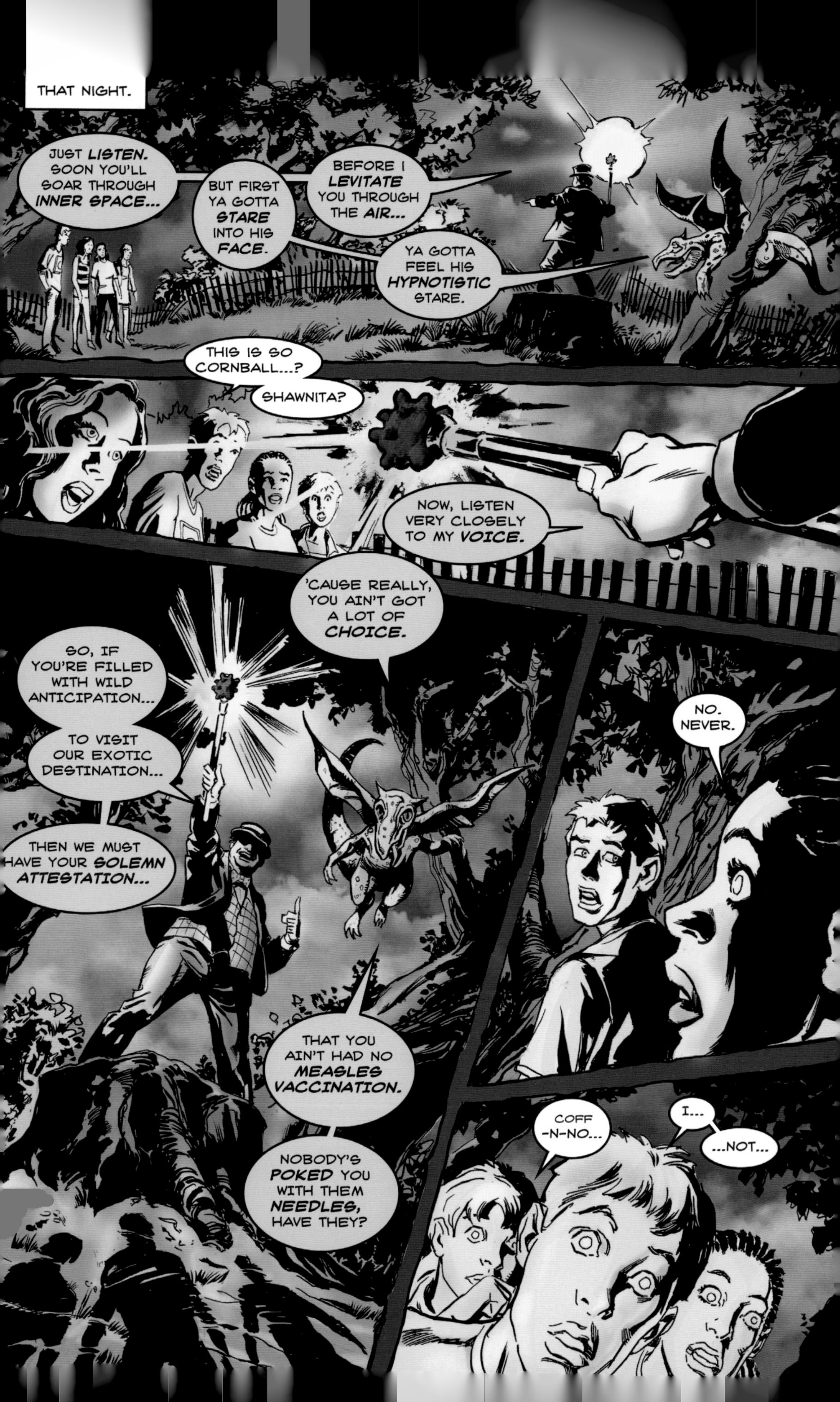
THAT NIGHT.
JUST LISTEN. SOON YOU'LL SOAR THROUGH INNER SPACE...
BUT FIRST YA GOTTA STARE INTO HIS FACE.
BEFORE I LEVITATE YOU THROUGH THE AIR...
YA GOTTA FEEL HIS HYPNOTISTIC STARE.
THIS IS SO CORNBALL...?
SHAWNITA?
NOW, LISTEN VERY CLOSELY TO MY VOICE.
'CAUSE REALLY, YOU AIN'T GOT A LOT OF CHOICE.
SO, IF YOU'RE FILLED WITH WILD ANTICIPATION...
TO VISIT OUR EXOTIC DESTINATION...
THEN WE MUST HAVE YOUR SOLEMN ATTESTATION...
THAT YOU AIN'T HAD NO MEASLES VACCINATION.
NOBODY'S POKED YOU WITH THEM NEEDLES, HAVE THEY?
NO. NEVER.
COFF -N-NO...
I...
...NOT...

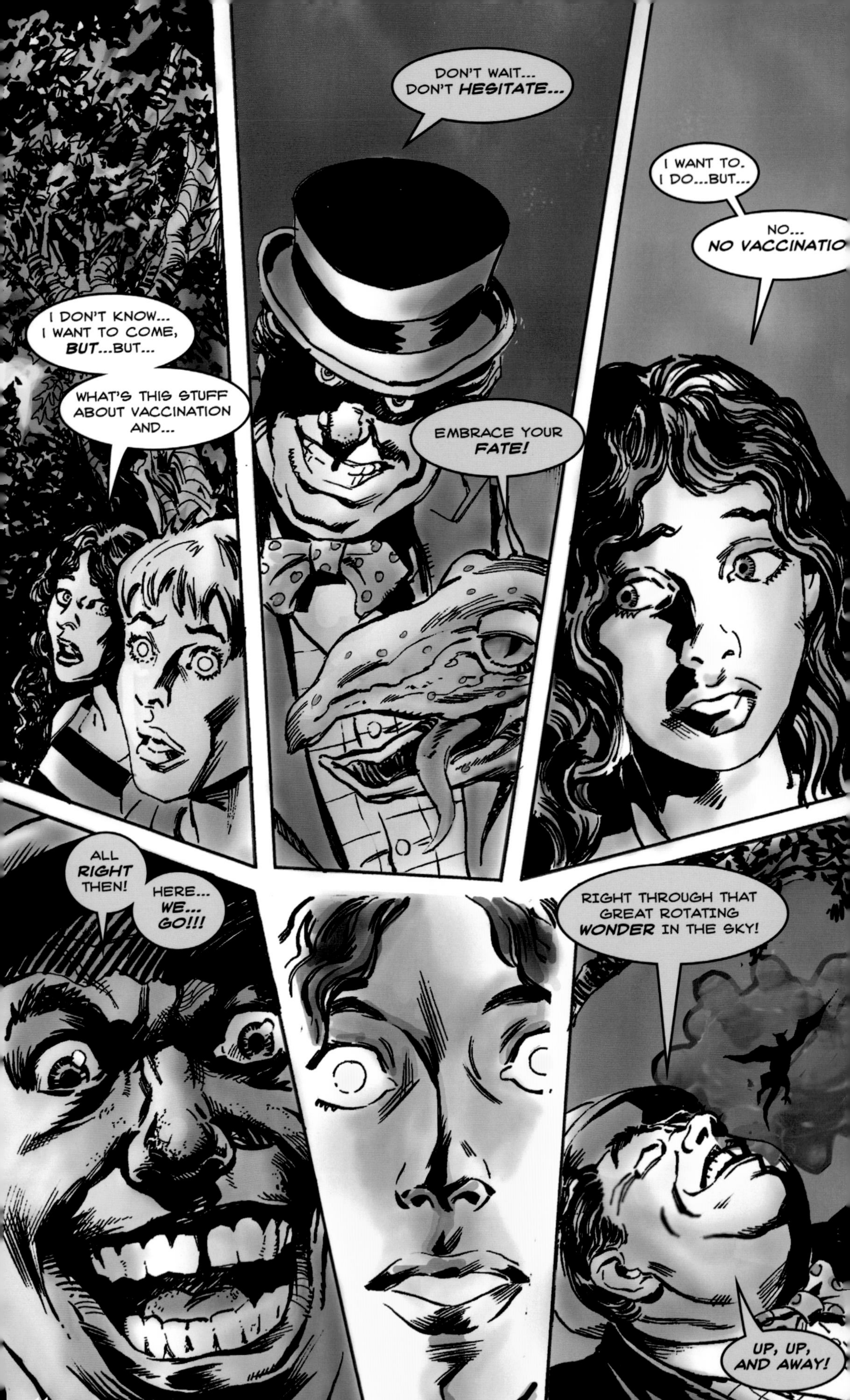
I DON'T KNOW... I WANT TO COME, BUT...BUT...
WHAT'S THIS STUFF ABOUT VACCINATION AND...
DON'T WAIT... DON'T HESITATE...
EMBRACE YOUR FATE!
I WANT TO. I DO...BUT...
NO... NO VACCINATIO
ALL RIGHT THEN!
HERE... WE... GO!!!
RIGHT THROUGH THAT GREAT ROTATING WONDER IN THE SKY!
UP, UP, AND AWAY!

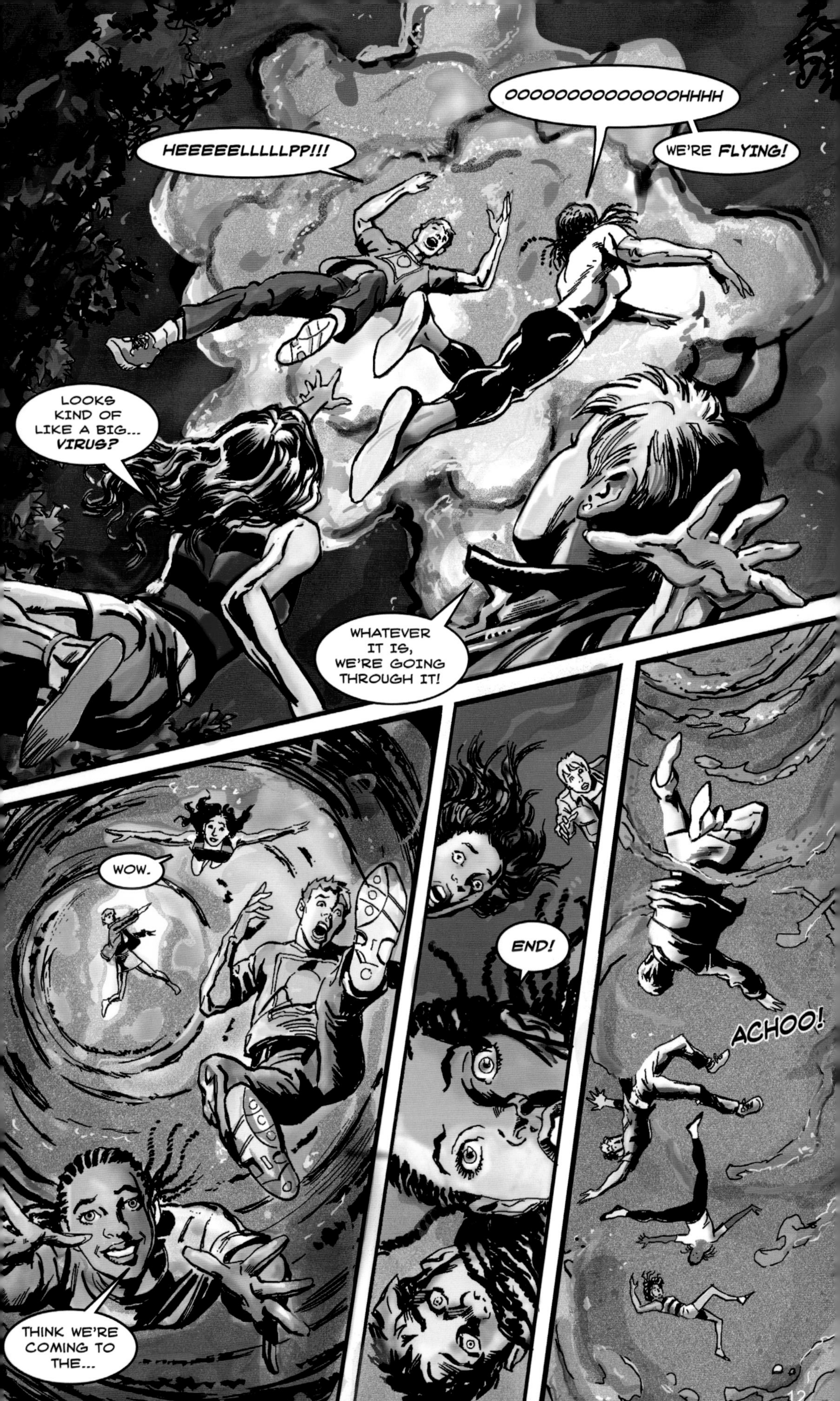

HEEEEEELLLLLPP!!!
OOOOOOOOOOOOOOHHHH
WE'RE FLYING!
LOOKS KIND OF LIKE A BIG... VIRUS?
WHATEVER IT IS, WE'RE GOING THROUGH IT!
WOW.
THINK WE'RE COMING TO THE...
END!
ACHOO!

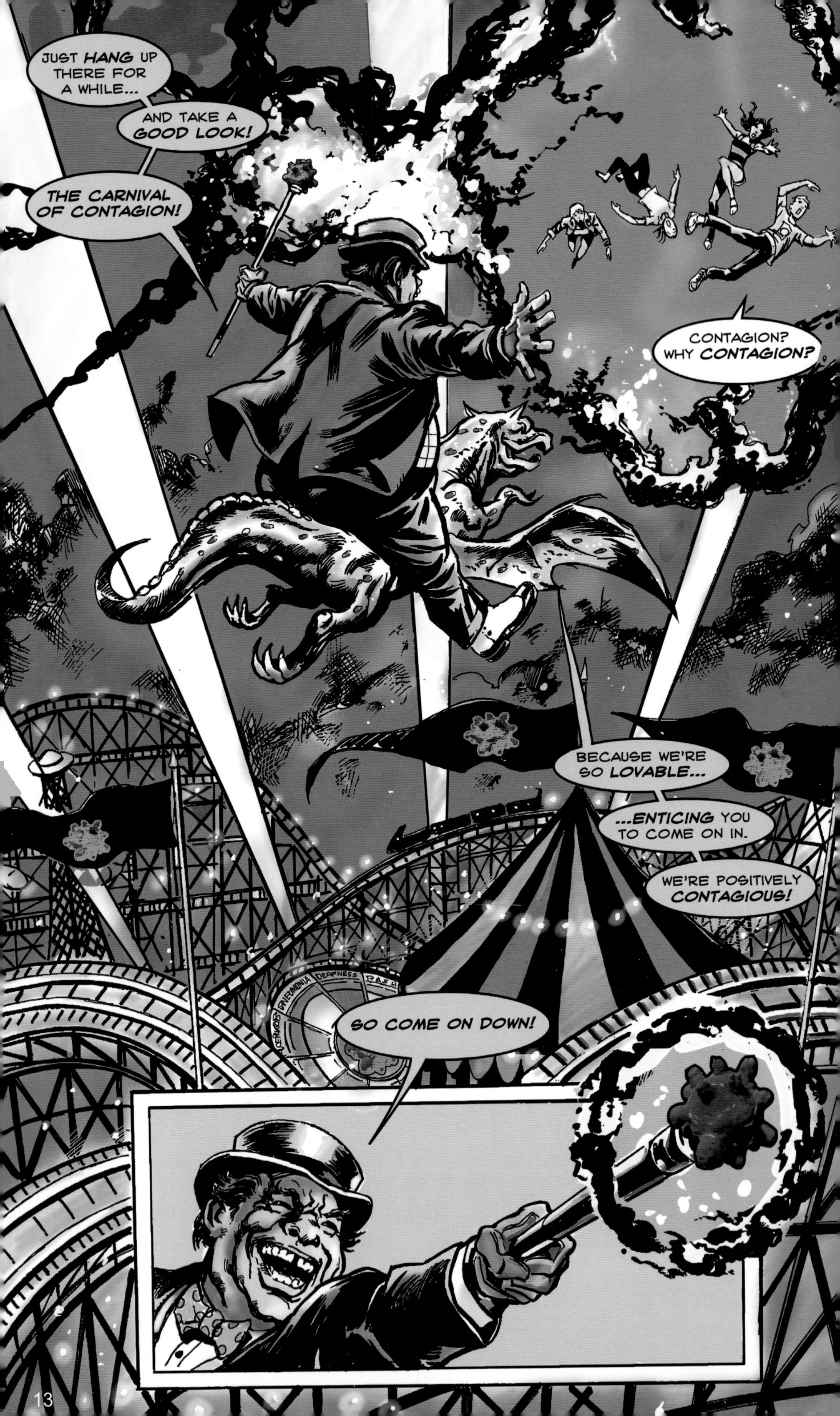
JUST HANG UP THERE FOR A WHILE...
AND TAKE A GOOD LOOK!
THE CARNIVAL OF CONTAGION!
CONTAGION? WHY CONTAGION?
BECAUSE WE'RE SO LOVABLE...
...ENTICING YOU TO COME ON IN.
WE'RE POSITIVELY CONTAGIOUS!
SO COME ON DOWN!

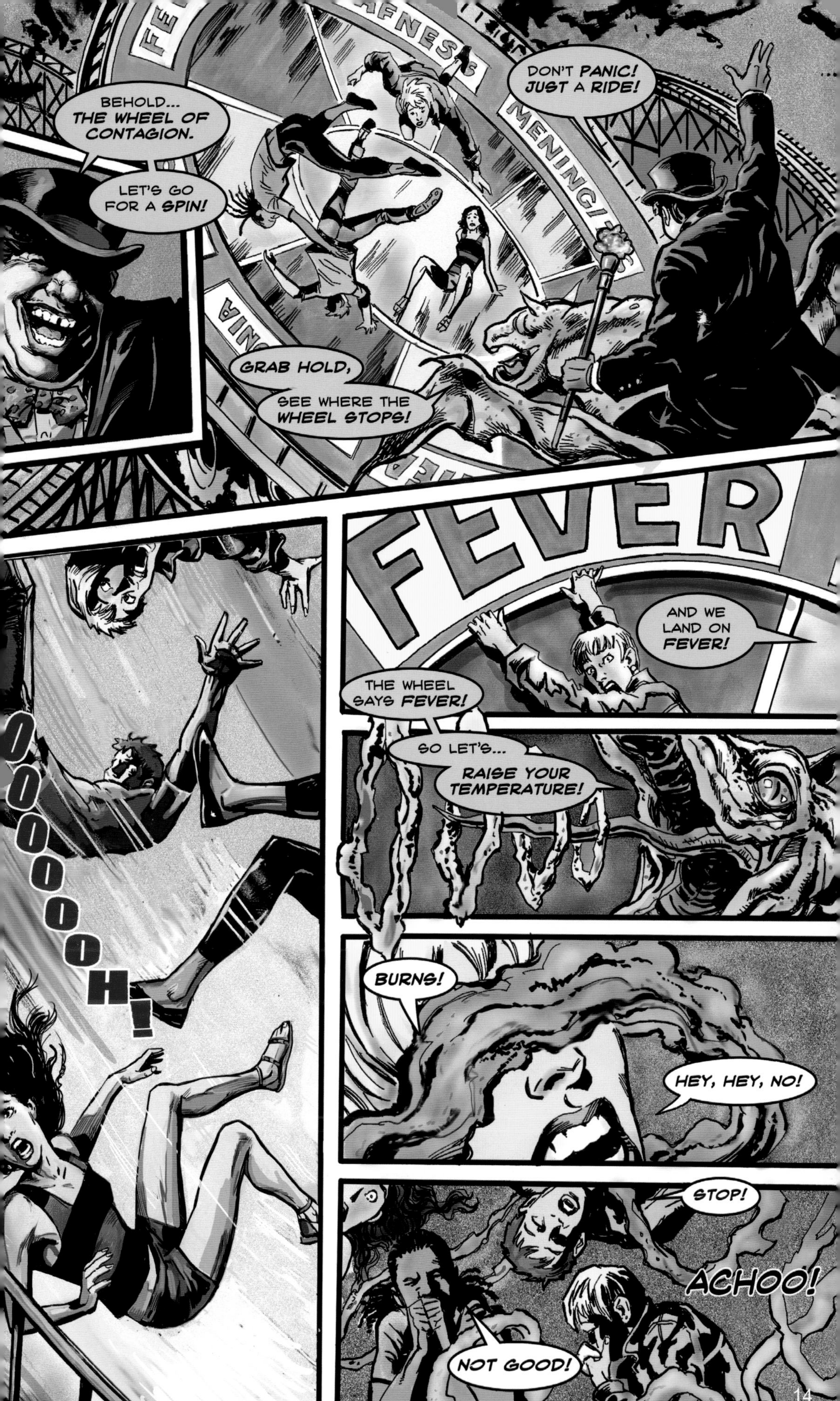
BEHOLD... THE WHEEL OF CONTAGION.
LET'S GO FOR A SPIN!
DON'T PANIC! JUST A RIDE!
GRAB HOLD,
SEE WHERE THE WHEEL STOPS!
FEVER
AND WE LAND ON FEVER!
OOOOOOOH!
THE WHEEL SAYS FEVER!
SO LET'S...
RAISE YOUR TEMPERATURE!
BURNS!
HEY, HEY, NO!
STOP!
ACHOO!
NOT GOOD!

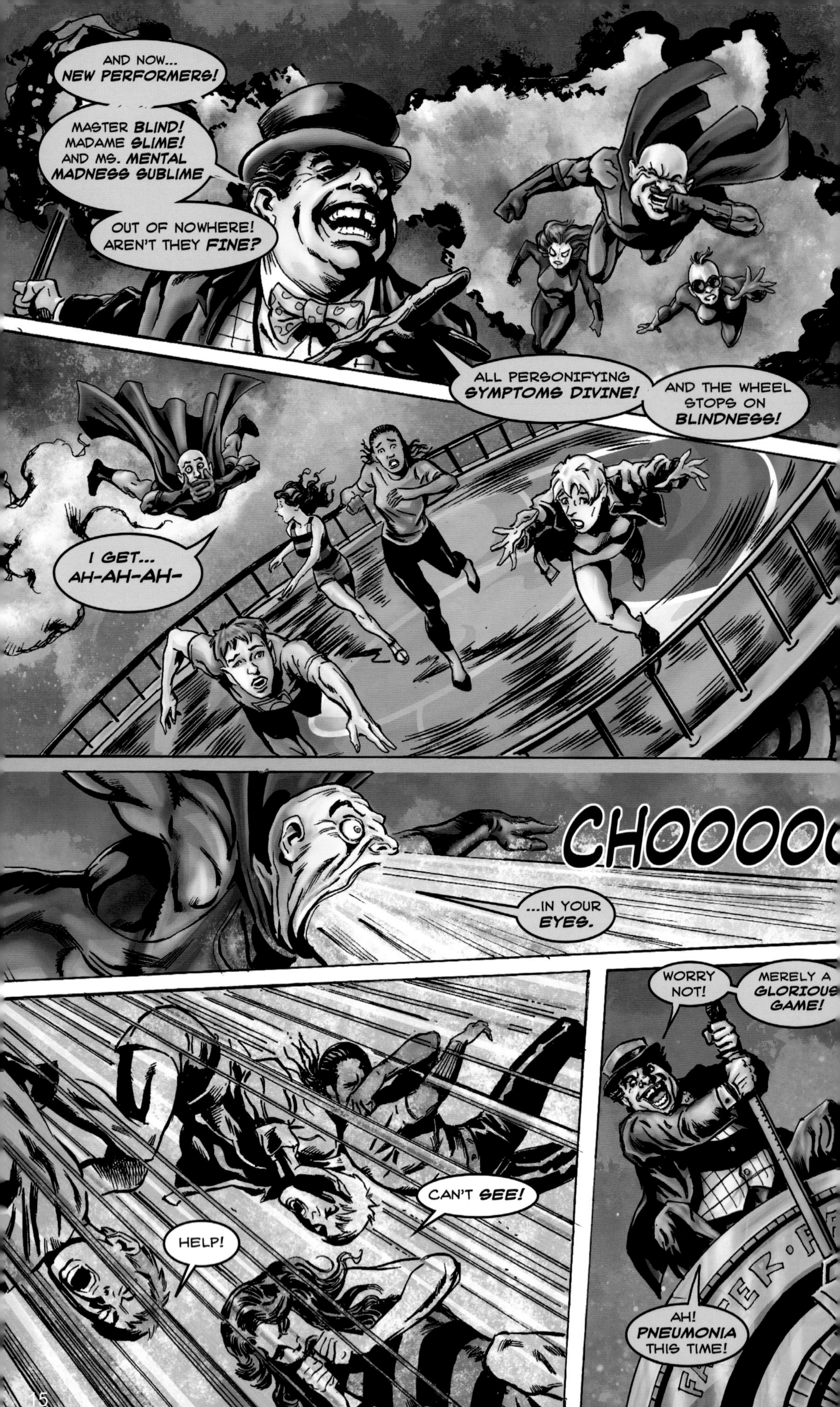
AND NOW... NEW PERFORMERS!
MASTER BLIND! MADAME SLIME! AND MS. MENTAL MADNESS SUBLIME
OUT OF NOWHERE! AREN'T THEY FINE?
ALL PERSONIFYING SYMPTOMS DIVINE!
AND THE WHEEL STOPS ON BLINDNESS!
I GET... AH-AH-AH-
CHOOOOO
...IN YOUR EYES.
WORRY NOT!
MERELY A GLORIOUS GAME!
CAN'T SEE!
HELP!
AH! PNEUMONIA THIS TIME!

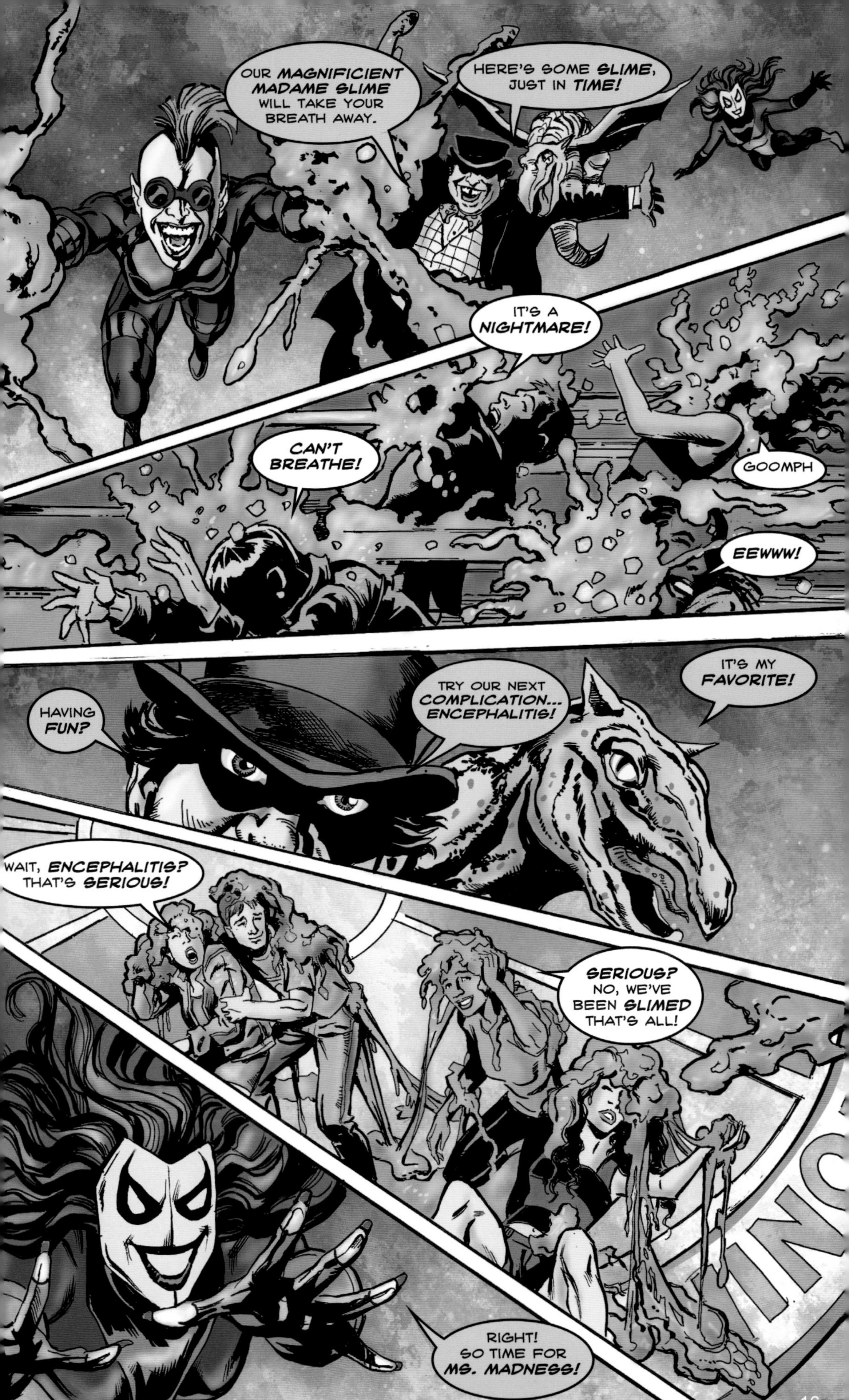
OUR MAGNIFICIENT MADAME SLIME WILL TAKE YOUR BREATH AWAY.
HERE'S SOME SLIME, JUST IN TIME!
IT'S A NIGHTMARE!
CAN'T BREATHE!
GOOMPH
EEWWW!
HAVING FUN?
TRY OUR NEXT COMPLICATION... ENCEPHALITIS!
IT'S MY FAVORITE!
WAIT, ENCEPHALITIS? THAT'S SERIOUS!
SERIOUS? NO, WE'VE BEEN SLIMED THAT'S ALL!
RIGHT! SO TIME FOR MS. MADNESS!

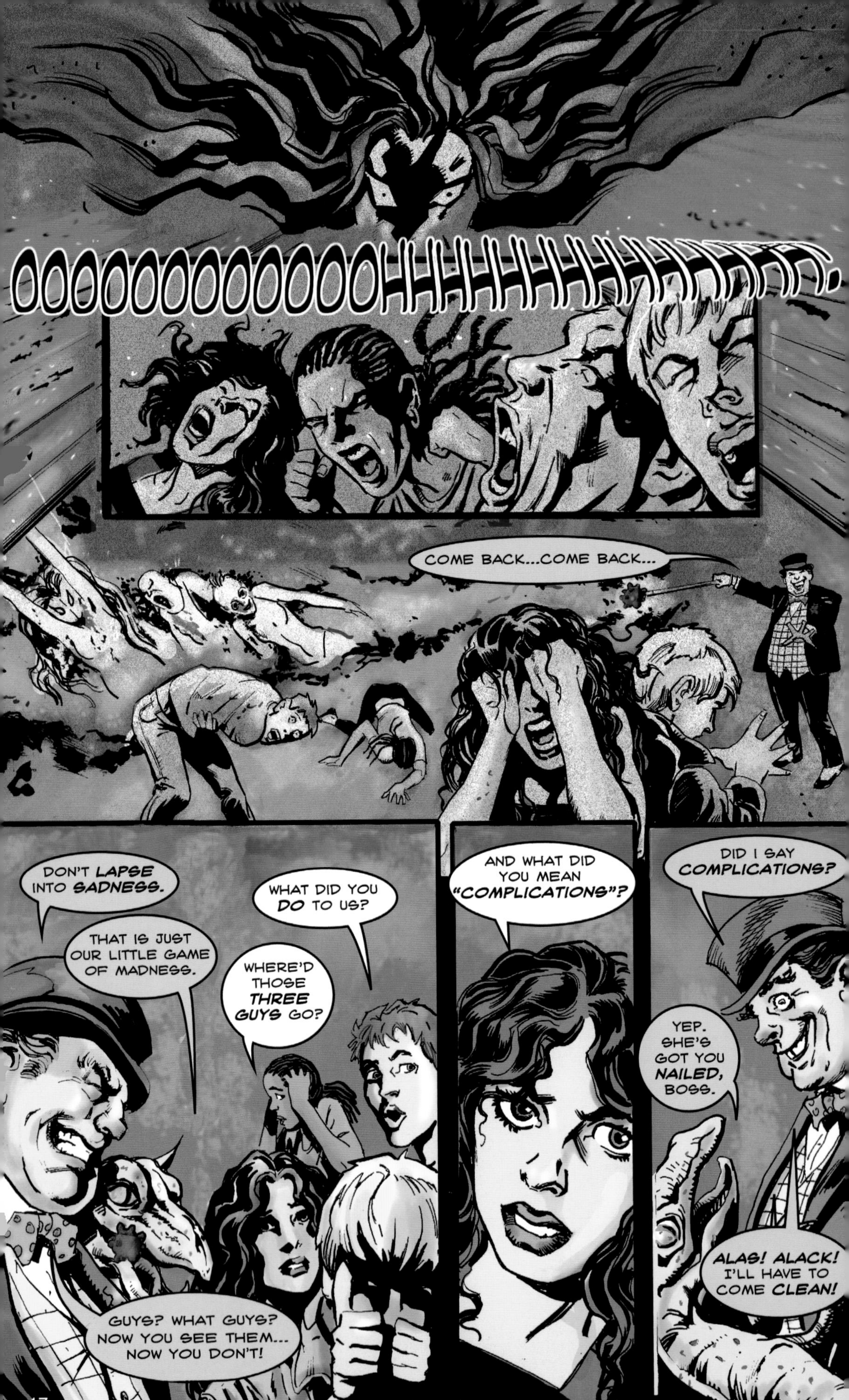
OOOOOOOOOOOOOHHHHHHHHHHHHHHH...
COME BACK...COME BACK...
DON'T LAPSE INTO SADNESS.
THAT IS JUST OUR LITTLE GAME OF MADNESS.
WHAT DID YOU DO TO US?
WHERE'D THOSE THREE GUYS GO?
GUYS? WHAT GUYS? NOW YOU SEE THEM... NOW YOU DON'T!
AND WHAT DID YOU MEAN "COMPLICATIONS"?
DID I SAY COMPLICATIONS?
YEP. SHE'S GOT YOU NAILED, BOSS.
ALAS! ALACK! I'LL HAVE TO COME CLEAN!

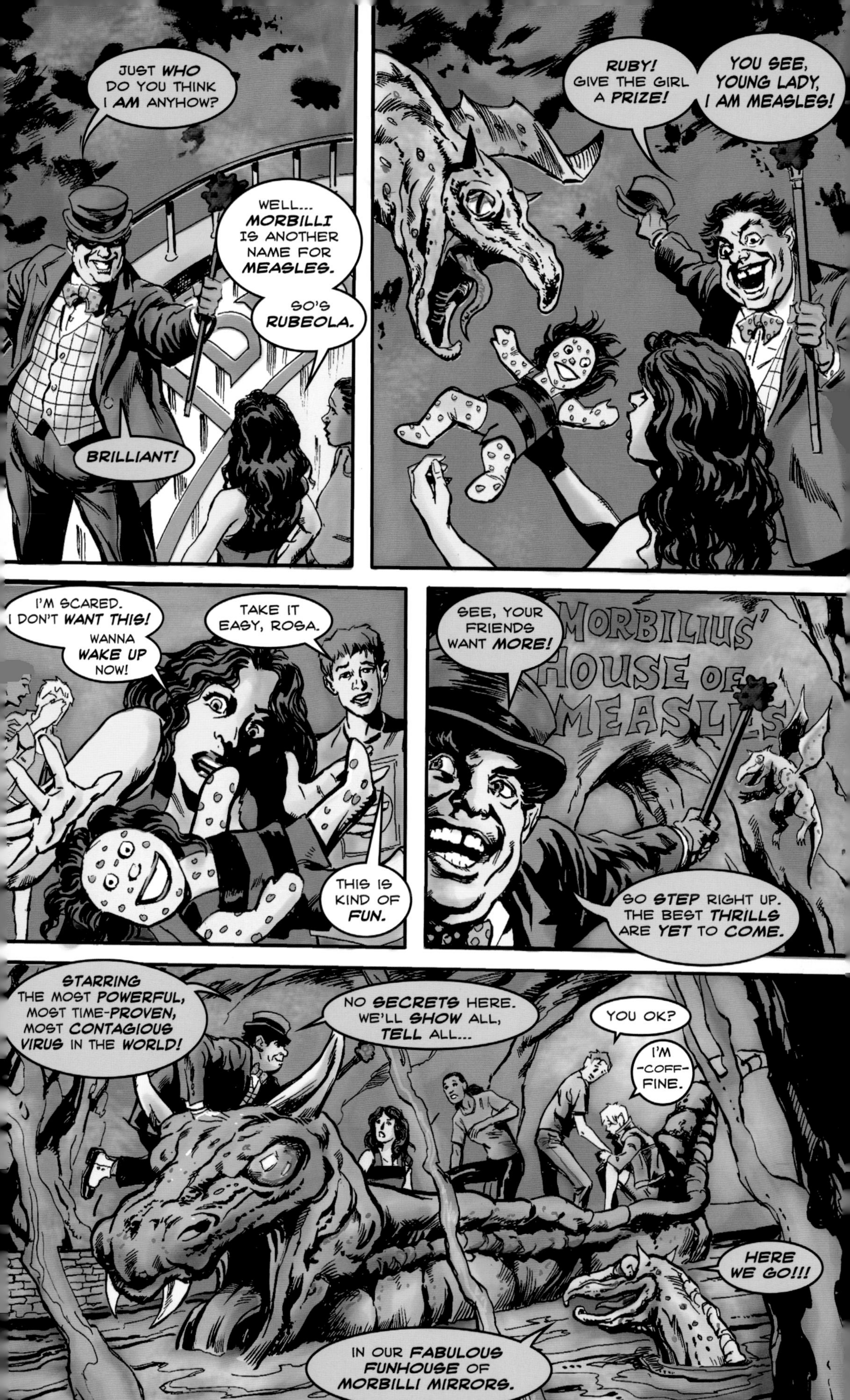
JUST WHO DO YOU THINK I AM ANYHOW?
WELL... MORBILLI IS ANOTHER NAME FOR MEASLES.
SO'S RUBEOLA.
BRILLIANT!
RUBY! GIVE THE GIRL A PRIZE!
YOU SEE, YOUNG LADY, I AM MEASLES!
I'M SCARED. I DON'T WANT THIS!
WANNA WAKE UP NOW!
TAKE IT EASY, ROSA.
THIS IS KIND OF FUN.
SEE, YOUR FRIENDS WANT MORE!
MORBILIUS' HOUSE OF MEASLES
SO STEP RIGHT UP. THE BEST THRILLS ARE YET TO COME.
STARRING THE MOST POWERFUL, MOST TIME-PROVEN, MOST CONTAGIOUS VIRUS IN THE WORLD!
NO SECRETS HERE. WE'LL SHOW ALL, TELL ALL...
YOU OK?
I'M -COFF- FINE.
HERE WE GO!!!
IN OUR FABULOUS FUNHOUSE OF MORBILLI MIRRORS.

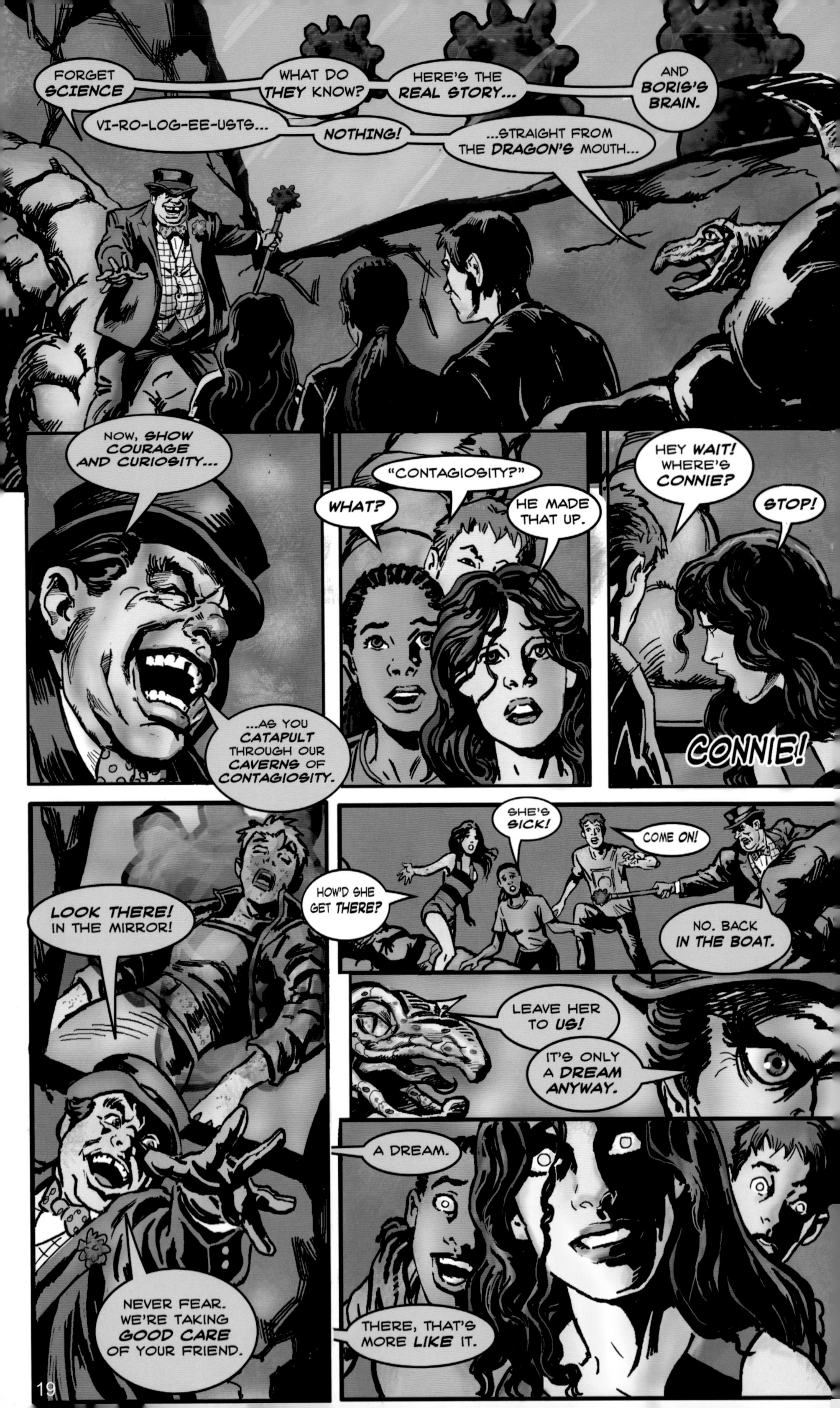

FORGET SCIENCE
VI-RO-LOG-EE-USTS...
WHAT DO THEY KNOW?
NOTHING!
HERE'S THE REAL STORY...
...STRAIGHT FROM THE DRAGON'S MOUTH...
AND BORIS'S BRAIN.
NOW, SHOW COURAGE AND CURIOSITY...
...AS YOU CATAPULT THROUGH OUR CAVERNS OF CONTAGIOSITY.
WHAT?
"CONTAGIOSITY?"
HE MADE THAT UP.
HEY WAIT! WHERE'S CONNIE?
STOP!
CONNIE!
LOOK THERE! IN THE MIRROR!
NEVER FEAR. WE'RE TAKING GOOD CARE OF YOUR FRIEND.
HOW'D SHE GET THERE?
SHE'S SICK!
COME ON!
NO. BACK IN THE BOAT.
LEAVE HER TO US!
IT'S ONLY A DREAM ANYWAY.
A DREAM.
THERE, THAT'S MORE LIKE IT.

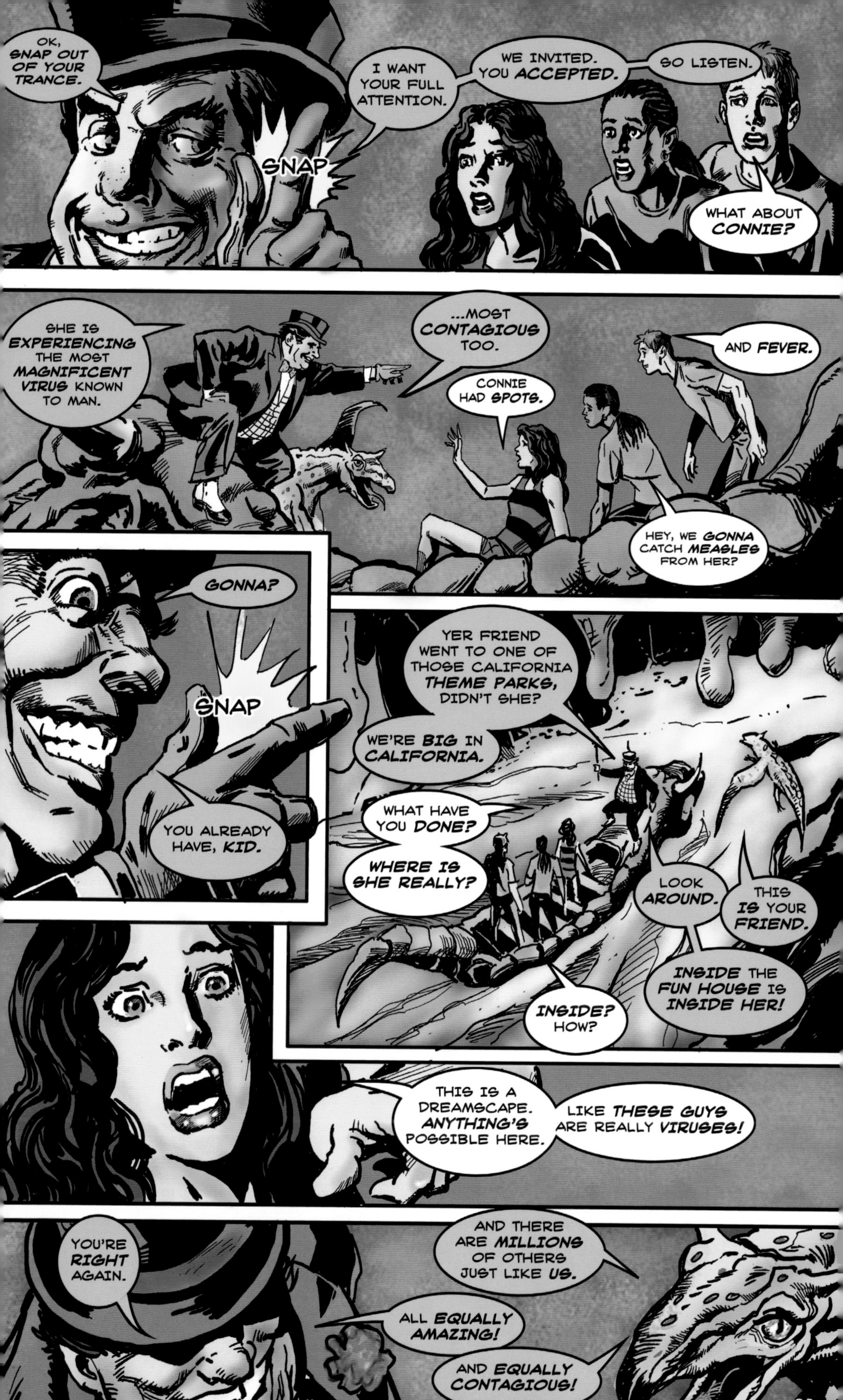

OK, SNAP OUT OF YOUR TRANCE.
SNAP
I WANT YOUR FULL ATTENTION.
WE INVITED. YOU ACCEPTED.
SO LISTEN.
WHAT ABOUT CONNIE?
SHE IS EXPERIENCING THE MOST MAGNIFICENT VIRUS KNOWN TO MAN.
...MOST CONTAGIOUS TOO.
CONNIE HAD SPOTS.
AND FEVER.
HEY, WE GONNA CATCH MEASLES FROM HER?
GONNA?
SNAP
YOU ALREADY HAVE, KID.
YER FRIEND WENT TO ONE OF THOSE CALIFORNIA THEME PARKS, DIDN'T SHE?
WE'RE BIG IN CALIFORNIA.
WHAT HAVE YOU DONE?
WHERE IS SHE REALLY?
LOOK AROUND.
THIS IS YOUR FRIEND.
INSIDE THE FUN HOUSE IS INSIDE HER!
INSIDE? HOW?
THIS IS A DREAMSCAPE. ANYTHING'S POSSIBLE HERE.
LIKE THESE GUYS ARE REALLY VIRUSES!
YOU'RE RIGHT AGAIN.
AND THERE ARE MILLIONS OF OTHERS JUST LIKE US.
ALL EQUALLY AMAZING!
AND EQUALLY CONTAGIOUS!

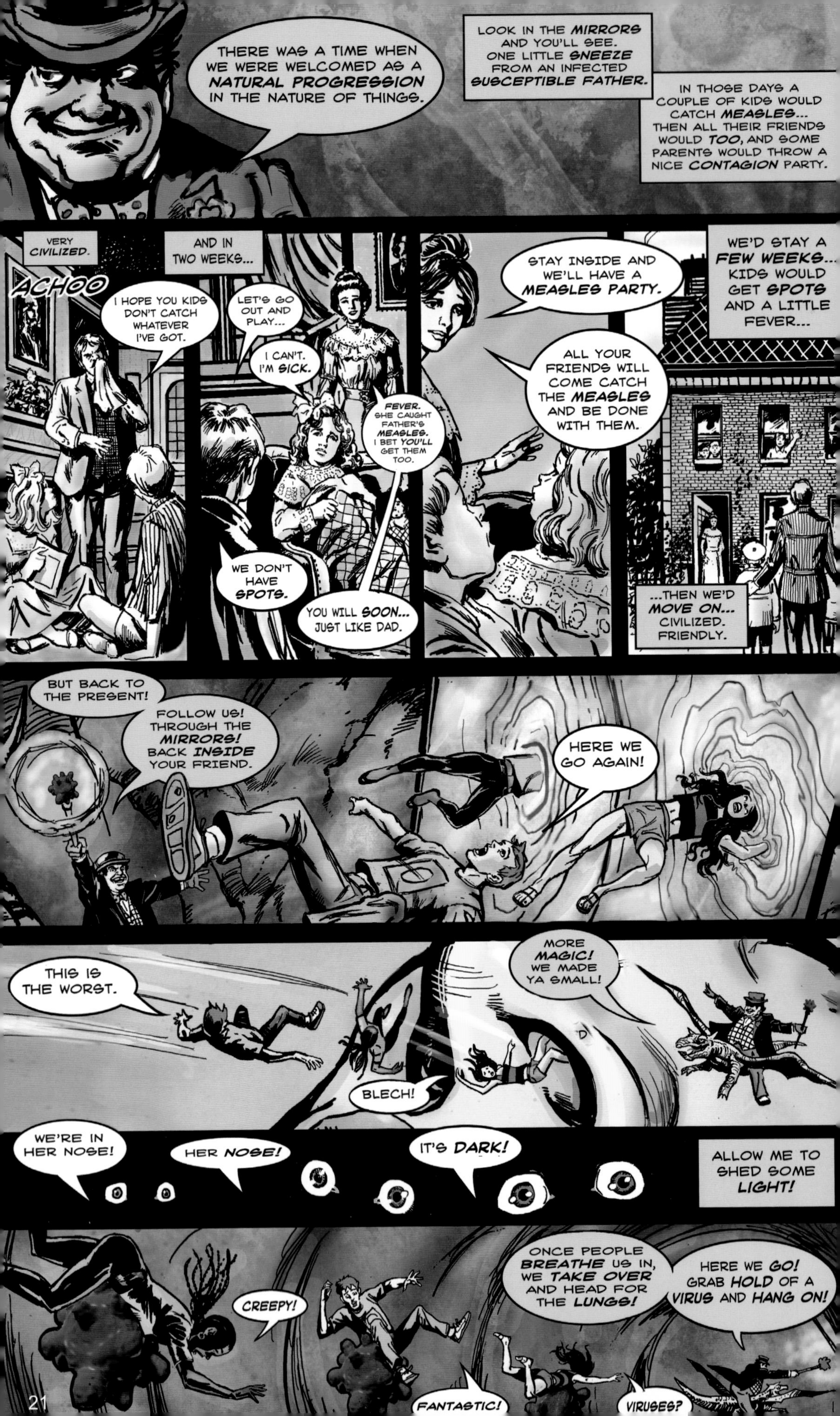
THERE WAS A TIME WHEN WE WERE WELCOMED AS A NATURAL PROGRESSION IN THE NATURE OF THINGS.
LOOK IN THE MIRRORS AND YOU'LL SEE. ONE LITTLE SNEEZE FROM AN INFECTED SUSCEPTIBLE FATHER.
IN THOSE DAYS A COUPLE OF KIDS WOULD CATCH MEASLES... THEN ALL THEIR FRIENDS WOULD TOO, AND SOME PARENTS WOULD THROW A NICE CONTAGION PARTY.
VERY CIVILIZED.
ACHOO
I HOPE YOU KIDS DON'T CATCH WHATEVER I'VE GOT.
AND IN TWO WEEKS...
LET'S GO OUT AND PLAY...
I CAN'T. I'M SICK.
FEVER. SHE CAUGHT FATHER'S MEASLES. I BET YOU'LL GET THEM TOO.
WE DON'T HAVE SPOTS.
YOU WILL SOON... JUST LIKE DAD.
STAY INSIDE AND WE'LL HAVE A MEASLES PARTY.
ALL YOUR FRIENDS WILL COME CATCH THE MEASLES AND BE DONE WITH THEM.
WE'D STAY A FEW WEEKS... KIDS WOULD GET SPOTS AND A LITTLE FEVER...
...THEN WE'D MOVE ON... CIVILIZED. FRIENDLY.
BUT BACK TO THE PRESENT!
FOLLOW US! THROUGH THE MIRRORS! BACK INSIDE YOUR FRIEND.
HERE WE GO AGAIN!
THIS IS THE WORST.
MORE MAGIC! WE MADE YA SMALL!
BLECH!
WE'RE IN HER NOSE!
HER NOSE!
IT'S DARK!
ALLOW ME TO SHED SOME LIGHT!
CREEPY!
ONCE PEOPLE BREATHE US IN, WE TAKE OVER AND HEAD FOR THE LUNGS!
HERE WE GO! GRAB HOLD OF A VIRUS AND HANG ON!
FANTASTIC!
VIRUSES?

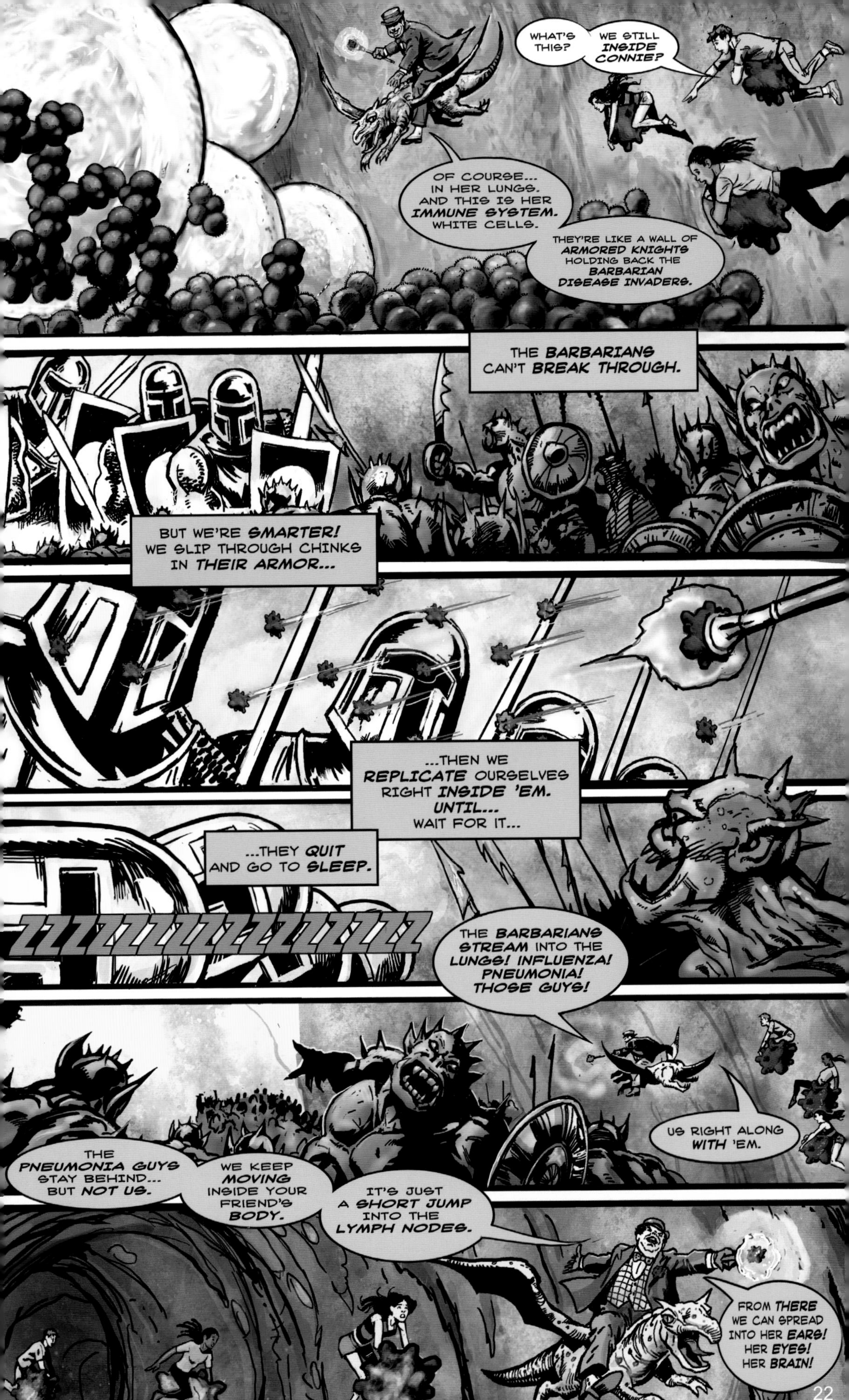
WHAT'S THIS?
WE STILL INSIDE CONNIE?
OF COURSE... IN HER LUNGS. AND THIS IS HER IMMUNE SYSTEM. WHITE CELLS.
THEY'RE LIKE A WALL OF ARMORED KNIGHTS HOLDING BACK THE BARBARIAN DISEASE INVADERS.
THE BARBARIANS CAN'T BREAK THROUGH.
BUT WE'RE SMARTER! WE SLIP THROUGH CHINKS IN THEIR ARMOR...
...THEN WE REPLICATE OURSELVES RIGHT INSIDE 'EM. UNTIL... WAIT FOR IT...
...THEY QUIT AND GO TO SLEEP.
ZZZZZZZZZZZZZZZZZZ
THE BARBARIANS STREAM INTO THE LUNGS! INFLUENZA! PNEUMONIA! THOSE GUYS!
US RIGHT ALONG WITH 'EM.
THE PNEUMONIA GUYS STAY BEHIND... BUT NOT US.
WE KEEP MOVING INSIDE YOUR FRIEND'S BODY.
IT'S JUST A SHORT JUMP INTO THE LYMPH NODES.
FROM THERE WE CAN SPREAD INTO HER EARS! HER EYES! HER BRAIN!

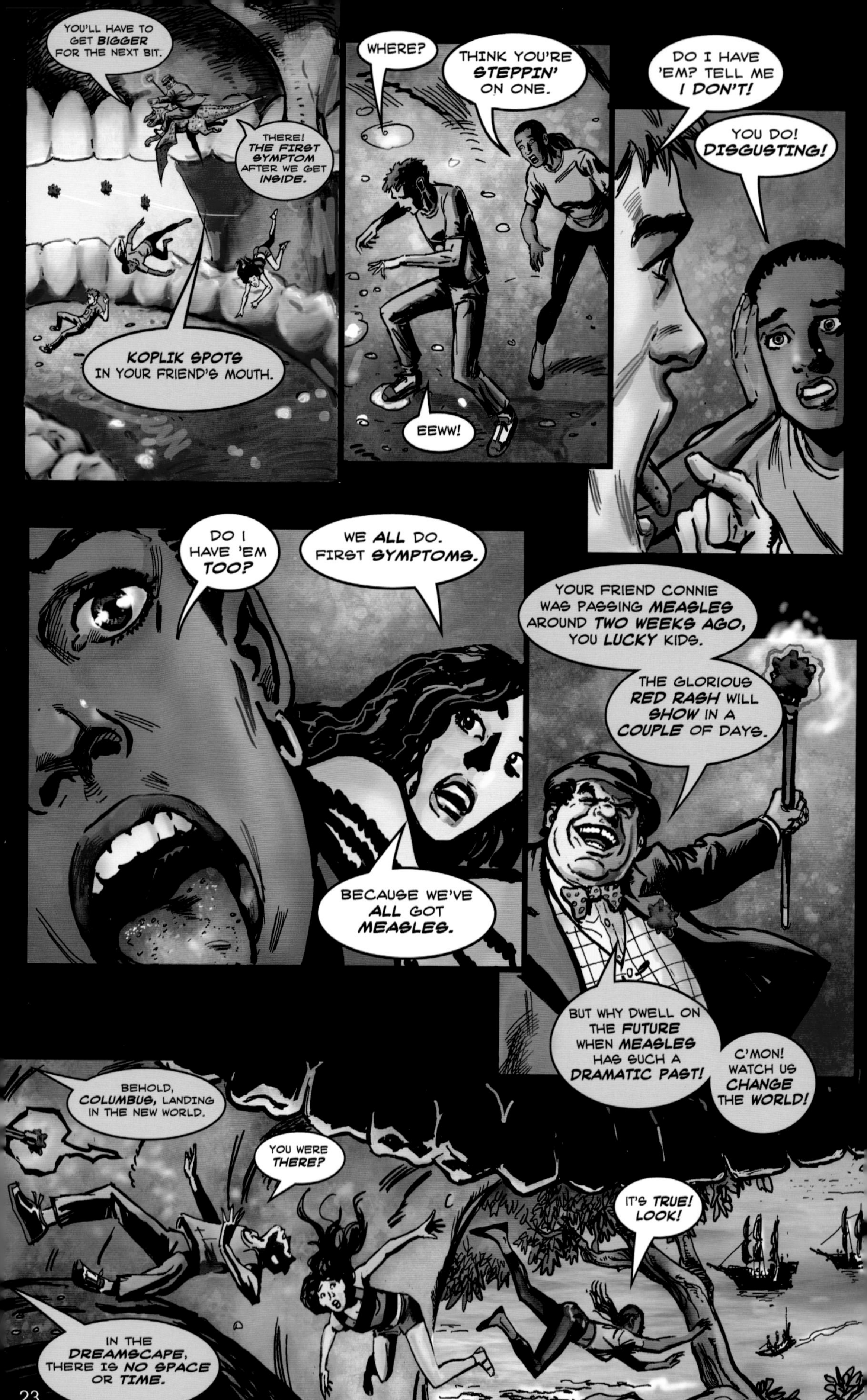
YOU'LL HAVE TO GET BIGGER FOR THE NEXT BIT.
THERE! THE FIRST SYMPTOM AFTER WE GET INSIDE.
KOPLIK SPOTS IN YOUR FRIEND'S MOUTH.
WHERE?
THINK YOU'RE STEPPIN' ON ONE.
EEWW!
DO I HAVE 'EM? TELL ME I DON'T!
YOU DO! DISGUSTING!
DO I HAVE 'EM TOO?
WE ALL DO. FIRST SYMPTOMS.
BECAUSE WE'VE ALL GOT MEASLES.
YOUR FRIEND CONNIE WAS PASSING MEASLES AROUND TWO WEEKS AGO, YOU LUCKY KIDS.
THE GLORIOUS RED RASH WILL SHOW IN A COUPLE OF DAYS.
BUT WHY DWELL ON THE FUTURE WHEN MEASLES HAS SUCH A DRAMATIC PAST!
C'MON! WATCH US CHANGE THE WORLD!
BEHOLD, COLUMBUS, LANDING IN THE NEW WORLD.
YOU WERE THERE?
IT'S TRUE! LOOK!
IN THE DREAMSCAPE, THERE IS NO SPACE OR TIME.

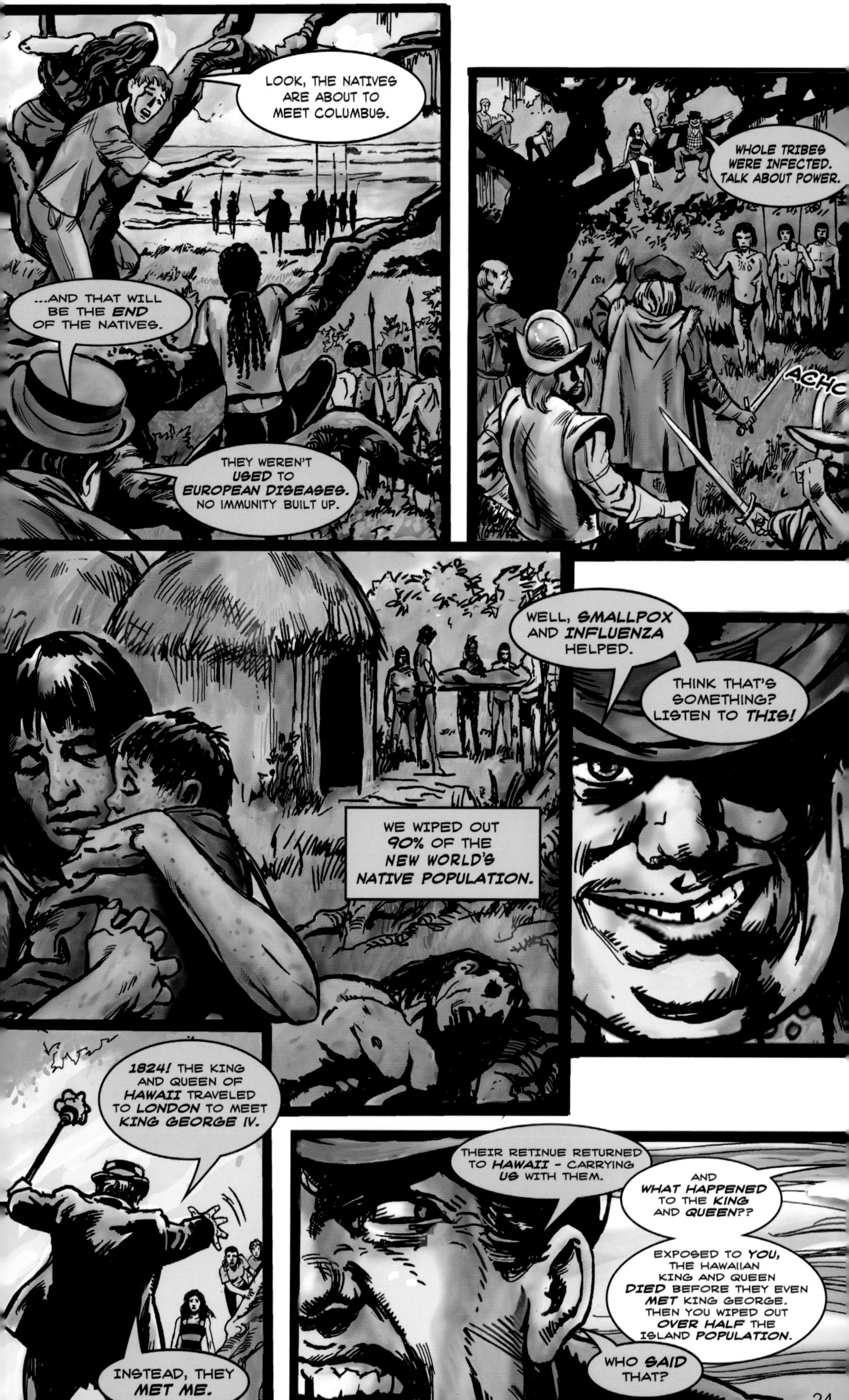
LOOK, THE NATIVES ARE ABOUT TO MEET COLUMBUS.
...AND THAT WILL BE THE END OF THE NATIVES.
THEY WEREN'T USED TO EUROPEAN DISEASES. NO IMMUNITY BUILT UP.
WHOLE TRIBES WERE INFECTED. TALK ABOUT POWER.
ACHO
WE WIPED OUT 90% OF THE NEW WORLD'S NATIVE POPULATION.
WELL, SMALLPOX AND INFLUENZA HELPED.
THINK THAT'S SOMETHING? LISTEN TO THIS!
1824! THE KING AND QUEEN OF HAWAII TRAVELED TO LONDON TO MEET KING GEORGE IV.
INSTEAD, THEY MET ME.
THEIR RETINUE RETURNED TO HAWAII - CARRYING US WITH THEM.
AND WHAT HAPPENED TO THE KING AND QUEEN??
EXPOSED TO YOU, THE HAWAIIAN KING AND QUEEN DIED BEFORE THEY EVEN MET KING GEORGE. THEN YOU WIPED OUT OVER HALF THE ISLAND POPULATION.
WHO SAID THAT?

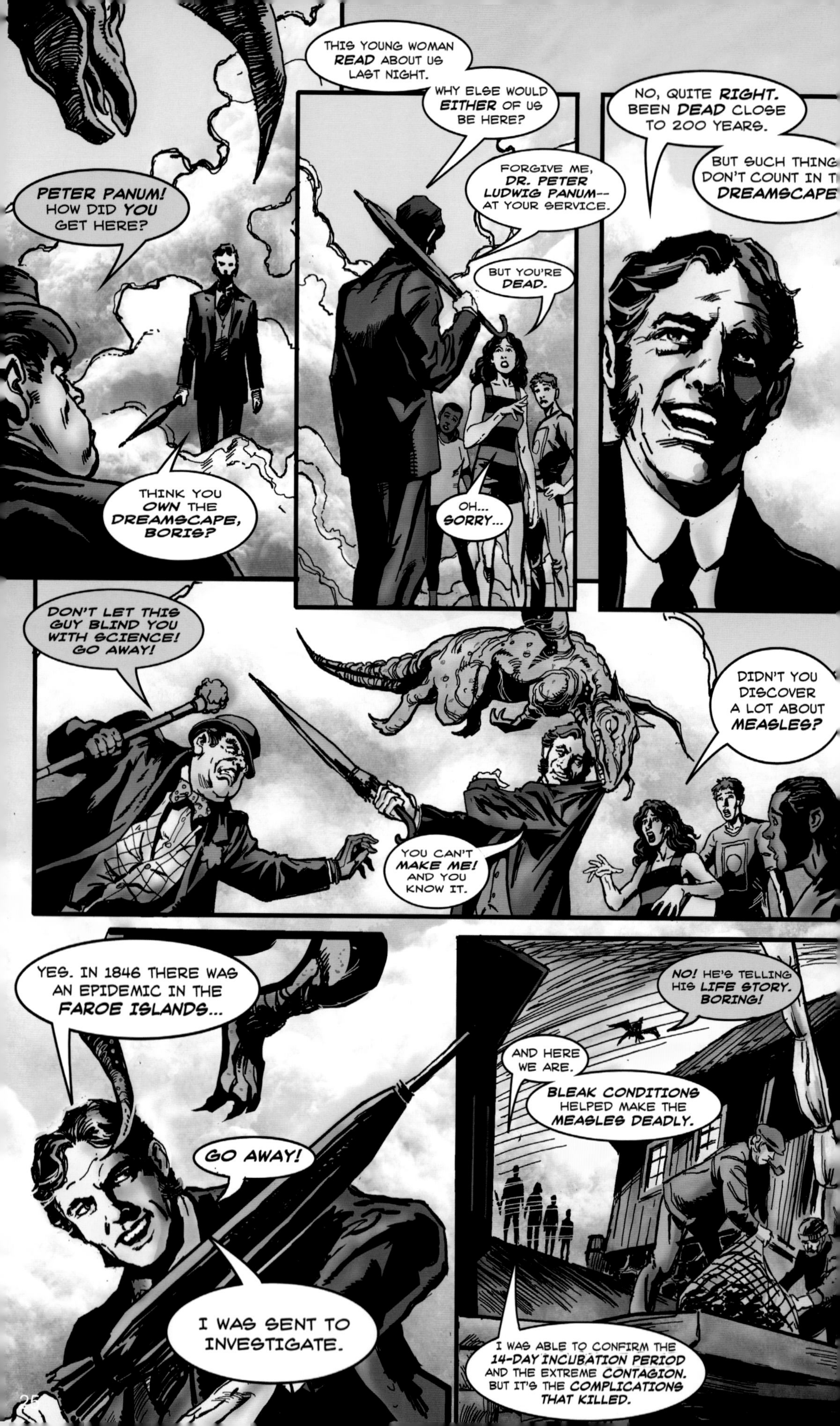
PETER PANUM! HOW DID YOU GET HERE?
THIS YOUNG WOMAN READ ABOUT US LAST NIGHT.
WHY ELSE WOULD EITHER OF US BE HERE?
FORGIVE ME, DR. PETER LUDWIG PANUM-- AT YOUR SERVICE.
BUT YOU'RE DEAD.
NO, QUITE RIGHT. BEEN DEAD CLOSE TO 200 YEARS.
BUT SUCH THING DON'T COUNT IN T DREAMSCAPE
THINK YOU OWN THE DREAMSCAPE, BORIS?
OH... SORRY...
DON'T LET THIS GUY BLIND YOU WITH SCIENCE! GO AWAY!
DIDN'T YOU DISCOVER A LOT ABOUT MEASLES?
YOU CAN'T MAKE ME! AND YOU KNOW IT.
YES. IN 1846 THERE WAS AN EPIDEMIC IN THE FAROE ISLANDS...
GO AWAY!
I WAS SENT TO INVESTIGATE.
NO! HE'S TELLING HIS LIFE STORY. BORING!
AND HERE WE ARE.
BLEAK CONDITIONS HELPED MAKE THE MEASLES DEADLY.
I WAS ABLE TO CONFIRM THE 14-DAY INCUBATION PERIOD AND THE EXTREME CONTAGION. BUT IT'S THE COMPLICATIONS THAT KILLED.

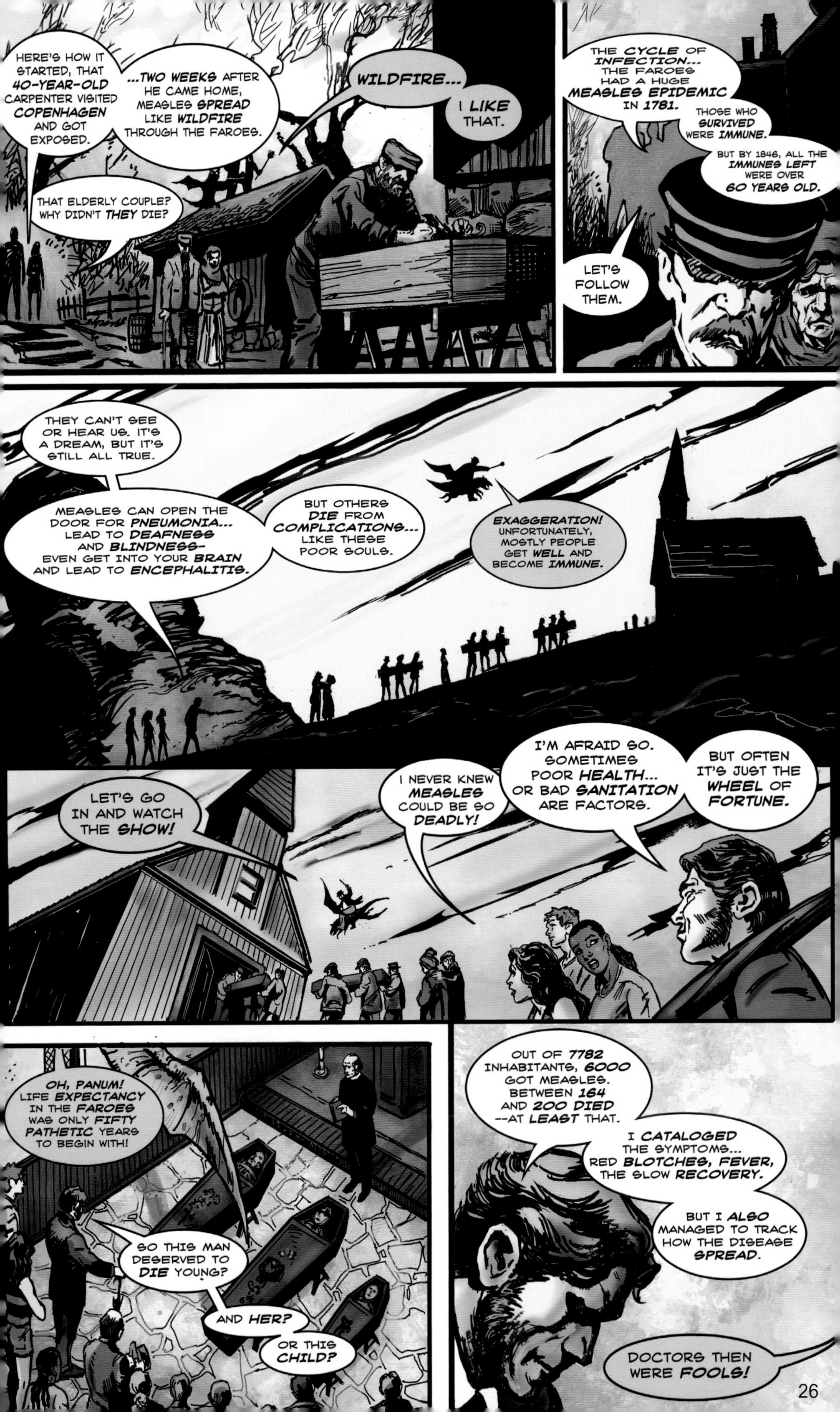
HERE'S HOW IT STARTED, THAT 40-YEAR-OLD CARPENTER VISITED COPENHAGEN AND GOT EXPOSED.
...TWO WEEKS AFTER HE CAME HOME, MEASLES SPREAD LIKE WILDFIRE THROUGH THE FAROES.
WILDFIRE...
I LIKE THAT.
THAT ELDERLY COUPLE? WHY DIDN'T THEY DIE?
THE CYCLE OF INFECTION... THE FAROES HAD A HUGE MEASLES EPIDEMIC IN 1781.
THOSE WHO SURVIVED WERE IMMUNE.
BUT BY 1846, ALL THE IMMUNES LEFT WERE OVER 60 YEARS OLD.
LET'S FOLLOW THEM.
THEY CAN'T SEE OR HEAR US. IT'S A DREAM, BUT IT'S STILL ALL TRUE.
MEASLES CAN OPEN THE DOOR FOR PNEUMONIA... LEAD TO DEAFNESS AND BLINDNESS– EVEN GET INTO YOUR BRAIN AND LEAD TO ENCEPHALITIS.
BUT OTHERS DIE FROM COMPLICATIONS... LIKE THESE POOR SOULS.
EXAGGERATION! UNFORTUNATELY, MOSTLY PEOPLE GET WELL AND BECOME IMMUNE.
LET'S GO IN AND WATCH THE SHOW!
I NEVER KNEW MEASLES COULD BE SO DEADLY!
I'M AFRAID SO. SOMETIMES POOR HEALTH... OR BAD SANITATION ARE FACTORS.
BUT OFTEN IT'S JUST THE WHEEL OF FORTUNE.
OH, PANUM! LIFE EXPECTANCY IN THE FAROES WAS ONLY FIFTY PATHETIC YEARS TO BEGIN WITH!
SO THIS MAN DESERVED TO DIE YOUNG?
AND HER?
OR THIS CHILD?
OUT OF 7782 INHABITANTS, 6000 GOT MEASLES. BETWEEN 164 AND 200 DIED --AT LEAST THAT.
I CATALOGED THE SYMPTOMS... RED BLOTCHES, FEVER, THE SLOW RECOVERY.
BUT I ALSO MANAGED TO TRACK HOW THE DISEASE SPREAD.
DOCTORS THEN WERE FOOLS!

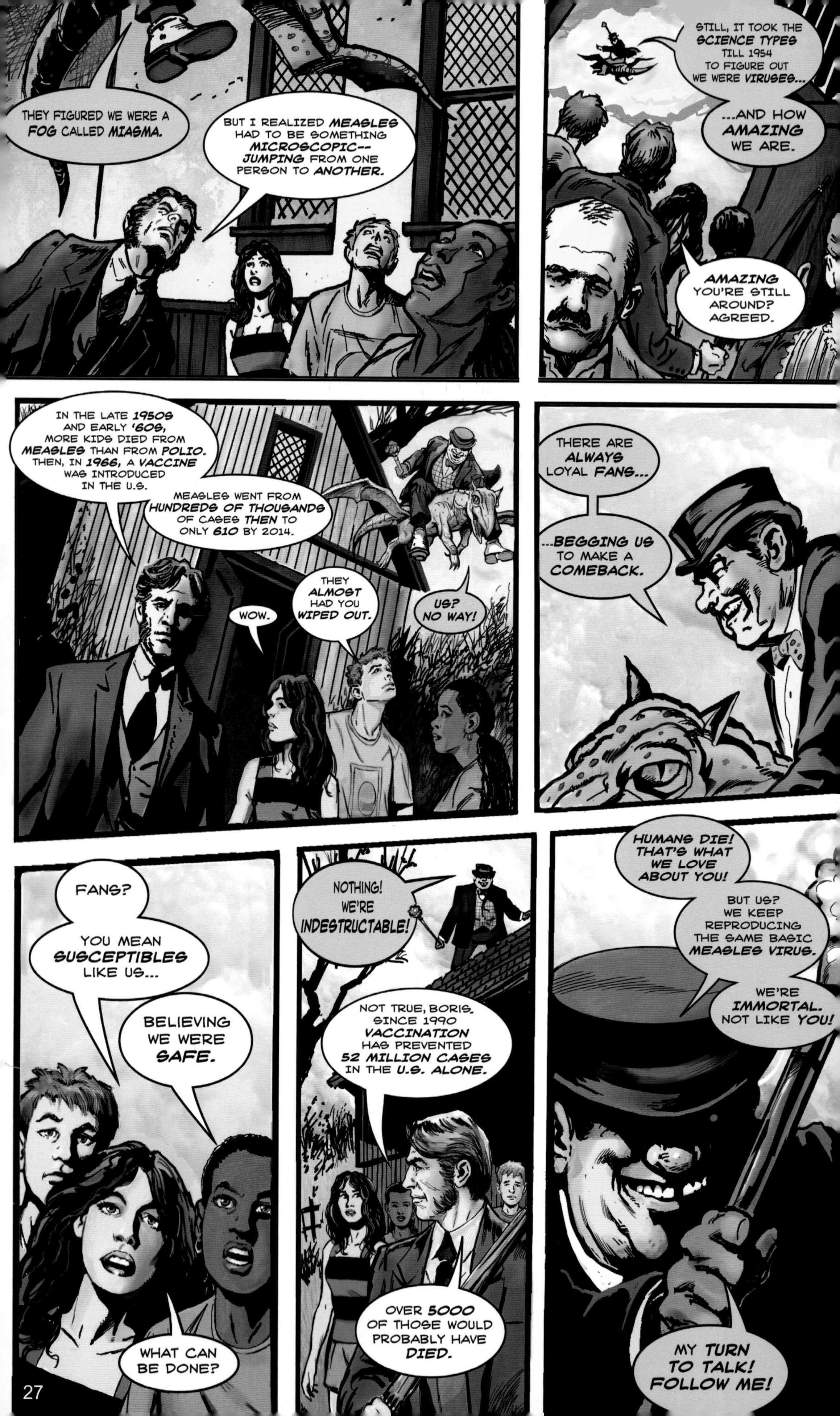
THEY FIGURED WE WERE A FOG CALLED MIASMA.
BUT I REALIZED MEASLES HAD TO BE SOMETHING MICROSCOPIC-- JUMPING FROM ONE PERSON TO ANOTHER.
STILL, IT TOOK THE SCIENCE TYPES TILL 1954 TO FIGURE OUT WE WERE VIRUSES...
...AND HOW AMAZING WE ARE.
AMAZING YOU'RE STILL AROUND? AGREED.
IN THE LATE 1950S AND EARLY '60S, MORE KIDS DIED FROM MEASLES THAN FROM POLIO. THEN, IN 1966, A VACCINE WAS INTRODUCED IN THE U.S.
MEASLES WENT FROM HUNDREDS OF THOUSANDS OF CASES THEN TO ONLY 610 BY 2014.
WOW.
THEY ALMOST HAD YOU WIPED OUT.
US? NO WAY!
THERE ARE ALWAYS LOYAL FANS...
...BEGGING US TO MAKE A COMEBACK.
FANS?
YOU MEAN SUSCEPTIBLES LIKE US...
BELIEVING WE WERE SAFE.
WHAT CAN BE DONE?
NOTHING! WE'RE INDESTRUCTABLE!
NOT TRUE, BORIS. SINCE 1990 VACCINATION HAS PREVENTED 52 MILLION CASES IN THE U.S. ALONE.
OVER 5000 OF THOSE WOULD PROBABLY HAVE DIED.
HUMANS DIE! THAT'S WHAT WE LOVE ABOUT YOU!
BUT US? WE KEEP REPRODUCING THE SAME BASIC MEASLES VIRUS.
WE'RE IMMORTAL. NOT LIKE YOU!
MY TURN TO TALK! FOLLOW ME!

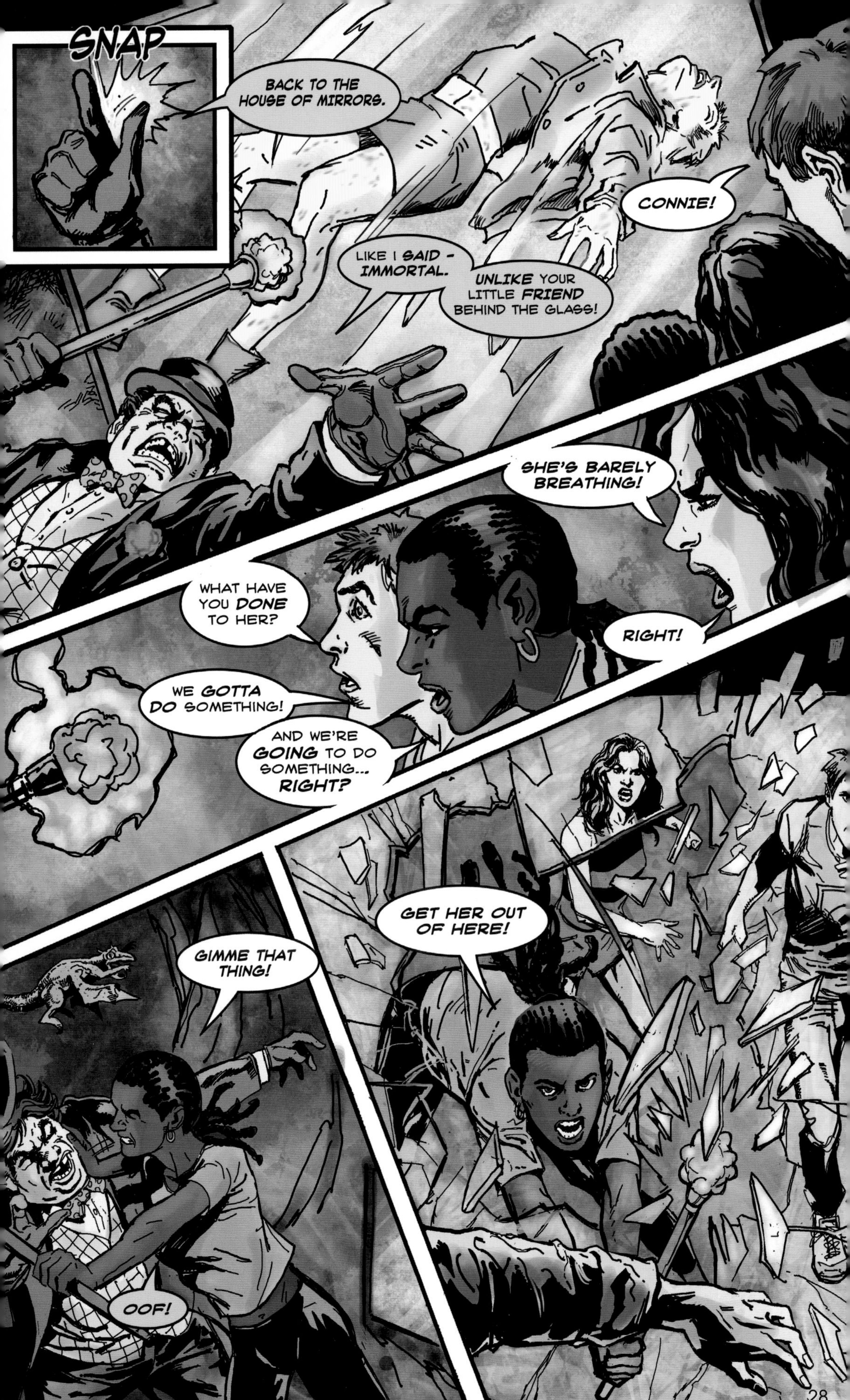
SNAP
BACK TO THE HOUSE OF MIRRORS.
CONNIE!
LIKE I SAID - IMMORTAL.
UNLIKE YOUR LITTLE FRIEND BEHIND THE GLASS!
SHE'S BARELY BREATHING!
WHAT HAVE YOU DONE TO HER?
RIGHT!
WE GOTTA DO SOMETHING!
AND WE'RE GOING TO DO SOMETHING... RIGHT?
GET HER OUT OF HERE!
GIMME THAT THING!
OOF!

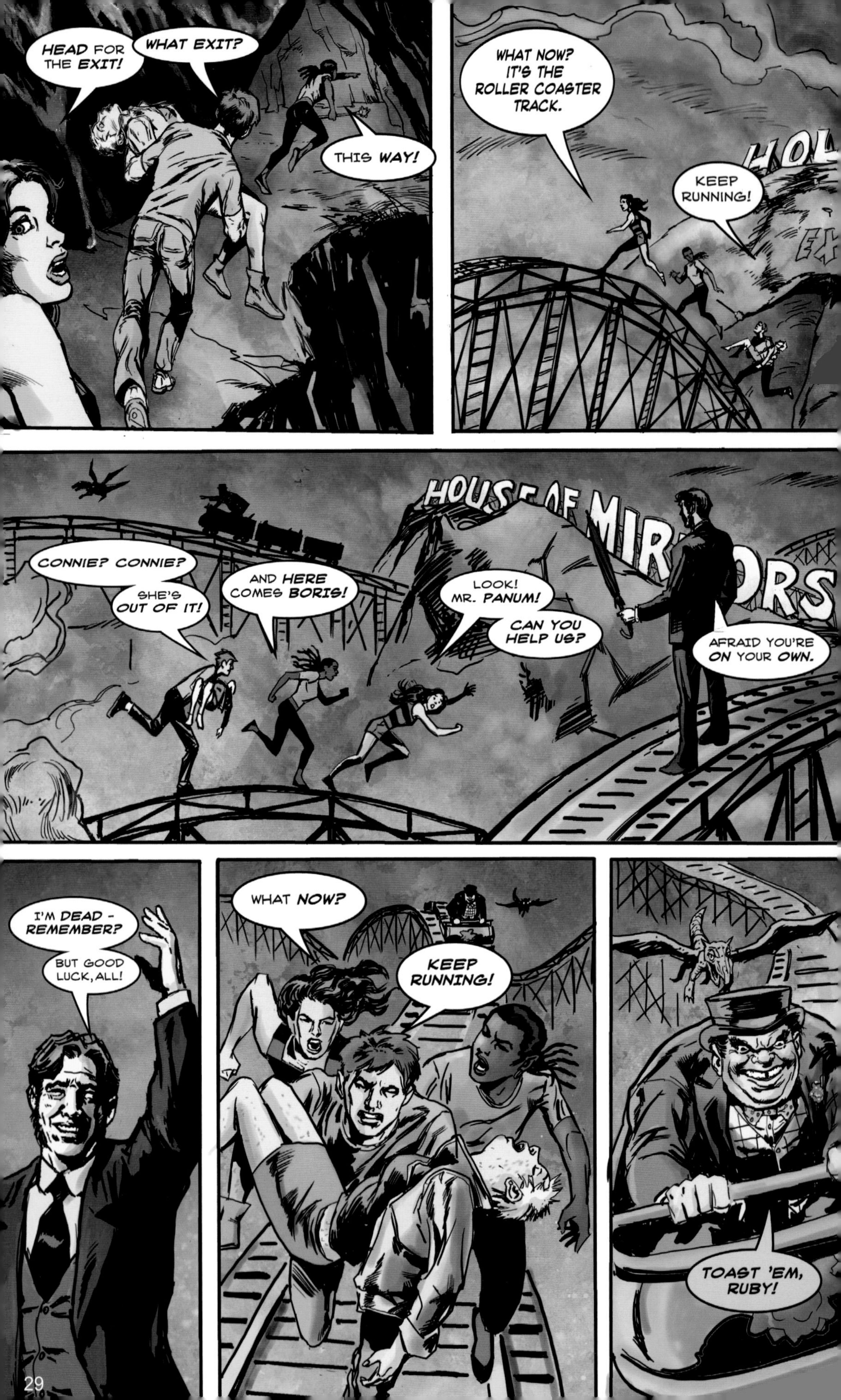
HEAD FOR THE EXIT!
WHAT EXIT?
THIS WAY!
WHAT NOW? IT'S THE ROLLER COASTER TRACK.
KEEP RUNNING!
HOUSE OF MIRRORS
CONNIE? CONNIE?
SHE'S OUT OF IT!
AND HERE COMES BORIS!
LOOK! MR. PANUM!
CAN YOU HELP US?
AFRAID YOU'RE ON YOUR OWN.
I'M DEAD - REMEMBER?
BUT GOOD LUCK, ALL!
WHAT NOW?
KEEP RUNNING!
TOAST 'EM, RUBY!

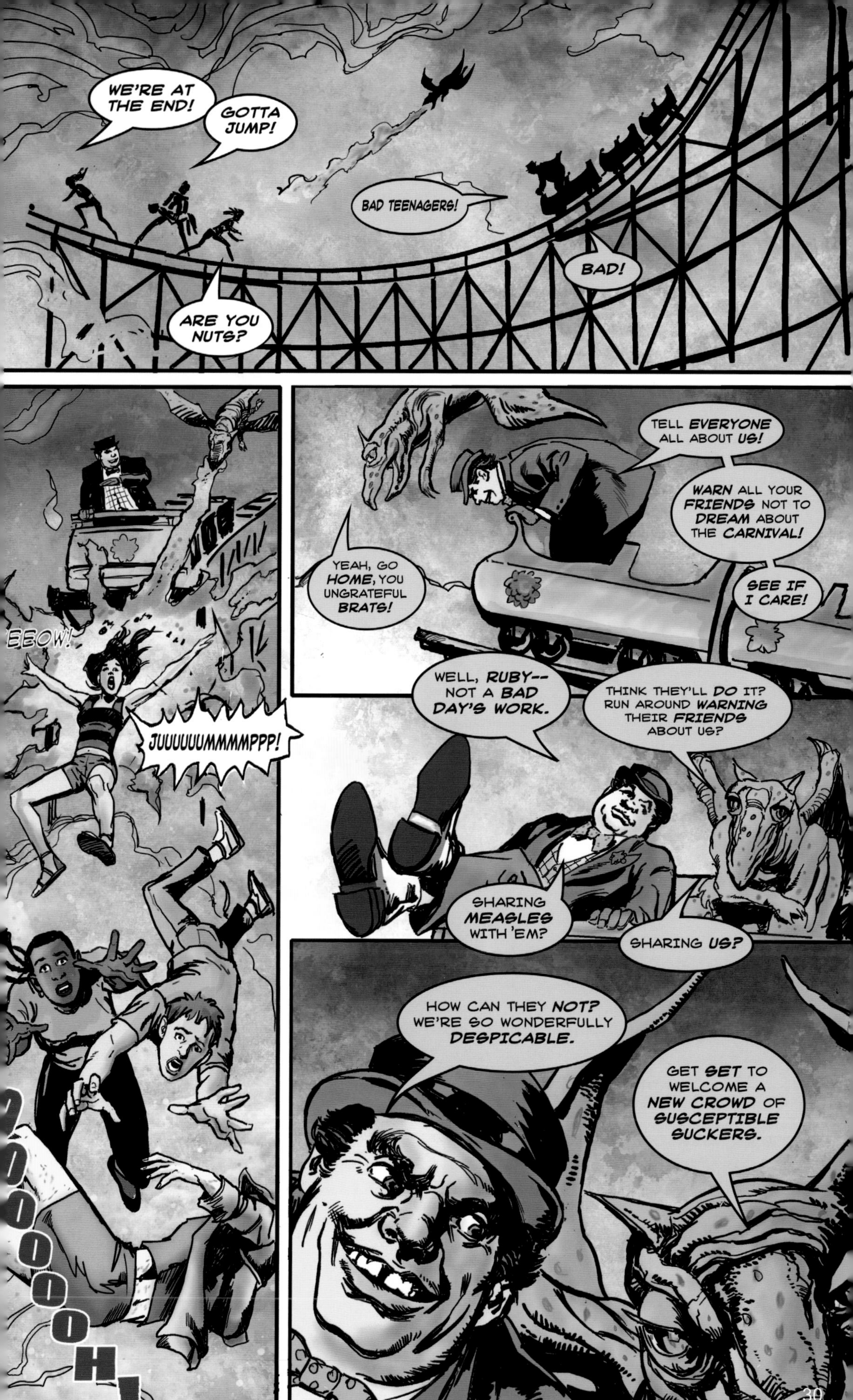

WE'RE AT THE END!
GOTTA JUMP!
BAD TEENAGERS!
ARE YOU NUTS?
BAD!
EEBOW!
JUUUUUUMMMMPPP!
OOOOOOOH!
TELL EVERYONE ALL ABOUT US!
WARN ALL YOUR FRIENDS NOT TO DREAM ABOUT THE CARNIVAL!
YEAH, GO HOME, YOU UNGRATEFUL BRATS!
SEE IF I CARE!
WELL, RUBY-- NOT A BAD DAY'S WORK.
THINK THEY'LL DO IT? RUN AROUND WARNING THEIR FRIENDS ABOUT US?
SHARING MEASLES WITH 'EM?
SHARING US?
HOW CAN THEY NOT? WE'RE SO WONDERFULLY DESPICABLE.
GET SET TO WELCOME A NEW CROWD OF SUSCEPTIBLE SUCKERS.

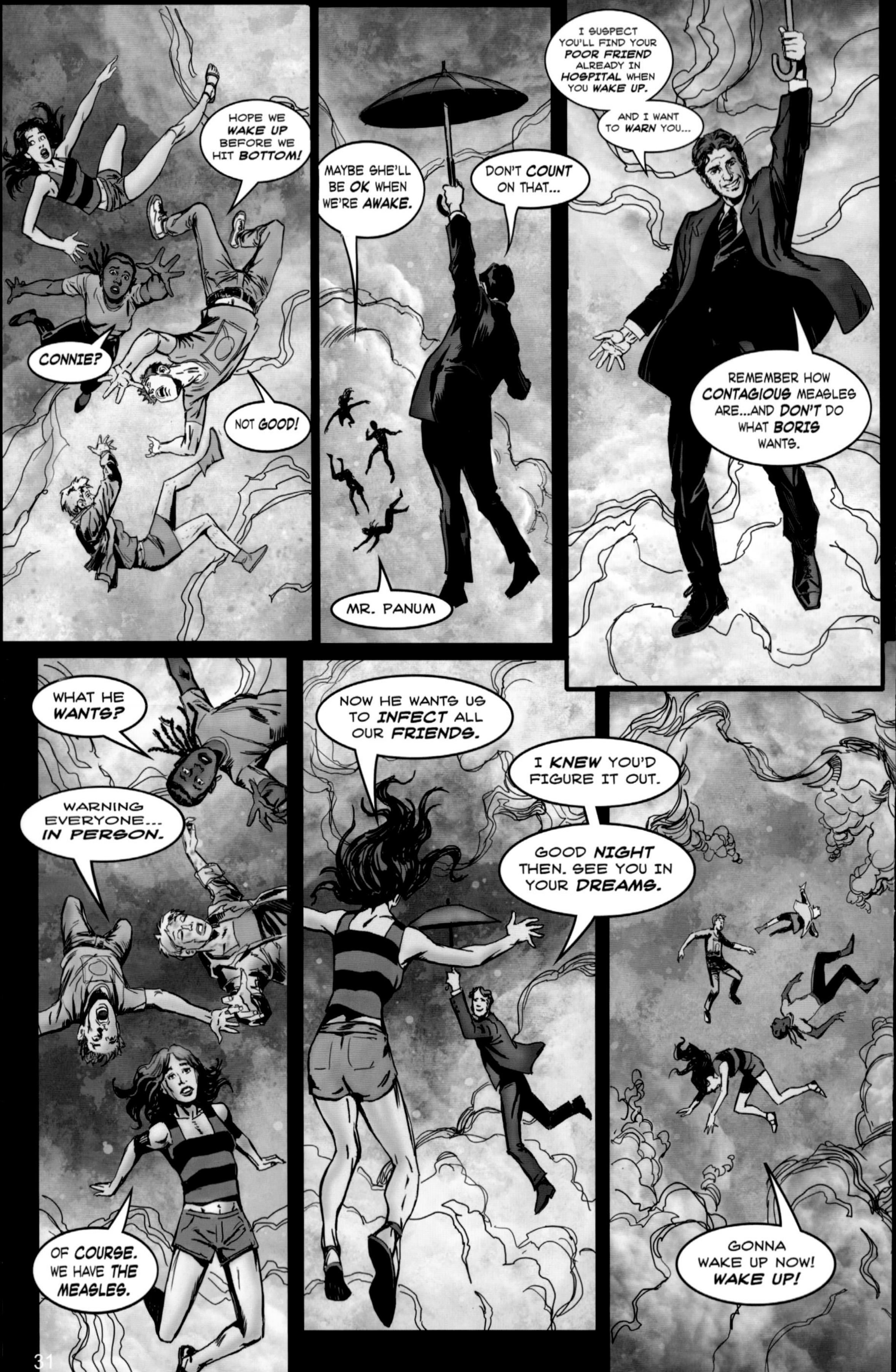
HOPE WE WAKE UP BEFORE WE HIT BOTTOM!
CONNIE?
NOT GOOD!
MAYBE SHE'LL BE OK WHEN WE'RE AWAKE.
DON'T COUNT ON THAT...
MR. PANUM
I SUSPECT YOU'LL FIND YOUR POOR FRIEND ALREADY IN HOSPITAL WHEN YOU WAKE UP.
AND I WANT TO WARN YOU...
REMEMBER HOW CONTAGIOUS MEASLES ARE...AND DON'T DO WHAT BORIS WANTS.
WHAT HE WANTS?
WARNING EVERYONE... IN PERSON.
OF COURSE. WE HAVE THE MEASLES.
NOW HE WANTS US TO INFECT ALL OUR FRIENDS.
I KNEW YOU'D FIGURE IT OUT.
GOOD NIGHT THEN. SEE YOU IN YOUR DREAMS.
GONNA WAKE UP NOW! WAKE UP!

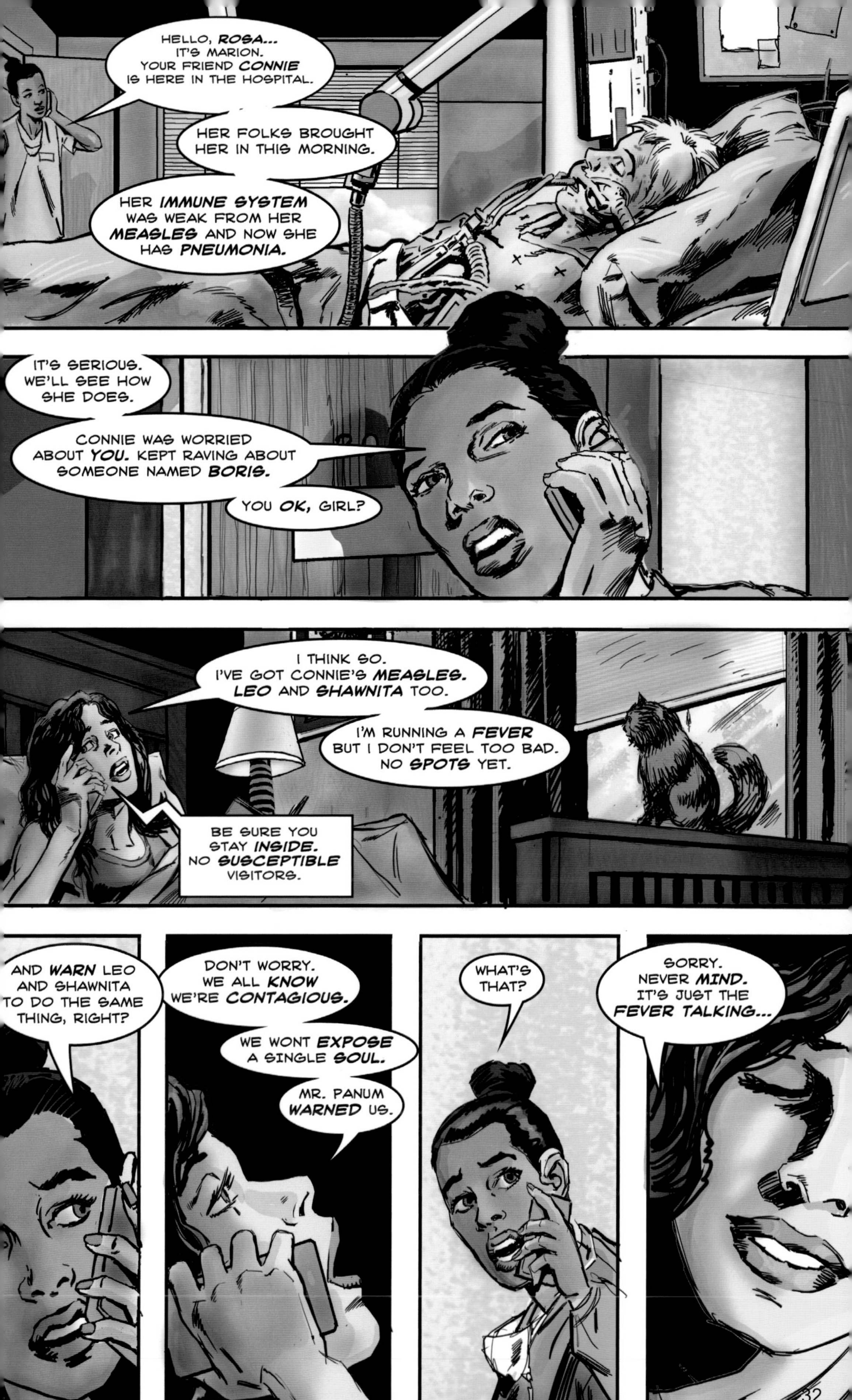
HELLO, ROSA... IT'S MARION. YOUR FRIEND CONNIE IS HERE IN THE HOSPITAL.
HER FOLKS BROUGHT HER IN THIS MORNING.
HER IMMUNE SYSTEM WAS WEAK FROM HER MEASLES AND NOW SHE HAS PNEUMONIA.
IT'S SERIOUS. WE'LL SEE HOW SHE DOES.
CONNIE WAS WORRIED ABOUT YOU. KEPT RAVING ABOUT SOMEONE NAMED BORIS.
YOU OK, GIRL?
I THINK SO. I'VE GOT CONNIE'S MEASLES. LEO AND SHAWNITA TOO.
I'M RUNNING A FEVER BUT I DON'T FEEL TOO BAD. NO SPOTS YET.
BE SURE YOU STAY INSIDE. NO SUSCEPTIBLE VISITORS.
AND WARN LEO AND SHAWNITA TO DO THE SAME THING, RIGHT?
DON'T WORRY. WE ALL KNOW WE'RE CONTAGIOUS.
WE WONT EXPOSE A SINGLE SOUL.
MR. PANUM WARNED US.
WHAT'S THAT?
SORRY. NEVER MIND. IT'S JUST THE FEVER TALKING...

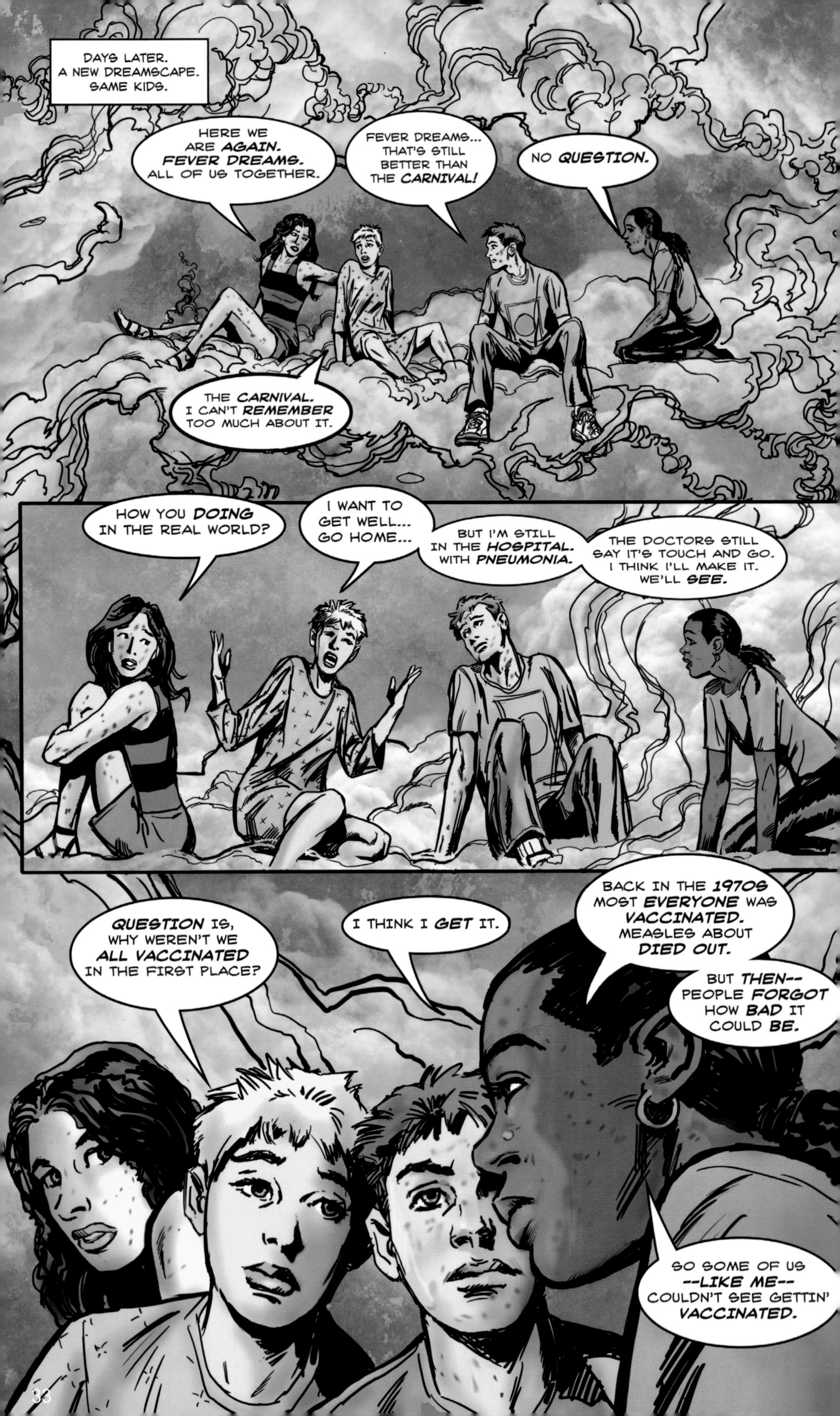
DAYS LATER.
A NEW DREAMSCAPE.
SAME KIDS.
HERE WE ARE AGAIN. FEVER DREAMS. ALL OF US TOGETHER.
FEVER DREAMS... THAT'S STILL BETTER THAN THE CARNIVAL!
NO QUESTION.
THE CARNIVAL. I CAN'T REMEMBER TOO MUCH ABOUT IT.
HOW YOU DOING IN THE REAL WORLD?
I WANT TO GET WELL... GO HOME...
BUT I'M STILL IN THE HOSPITAL. WITH PNEUMONIA.
THE DOCTORS STILL SAY IT'S TOUCH AND GO. I THINK I'LL MAKE IT. WE'LL SEE.
QUESTION IS, WHY WEREN'T WE ALL VACCINATED IN THE FIRST PLACE?
I THINK I GET IT.
BACK IN THE 1970S MOST EVERYONE WAS VACCINATED. MEASLES ABOUT DIED OUT.
BUT THEN-- PEOPLE FORGOT HOW BAD IT COULD BE.
SO SOME OF US --LIKE ME-- COULDN'T SEE GETTIN' VACCINATED.

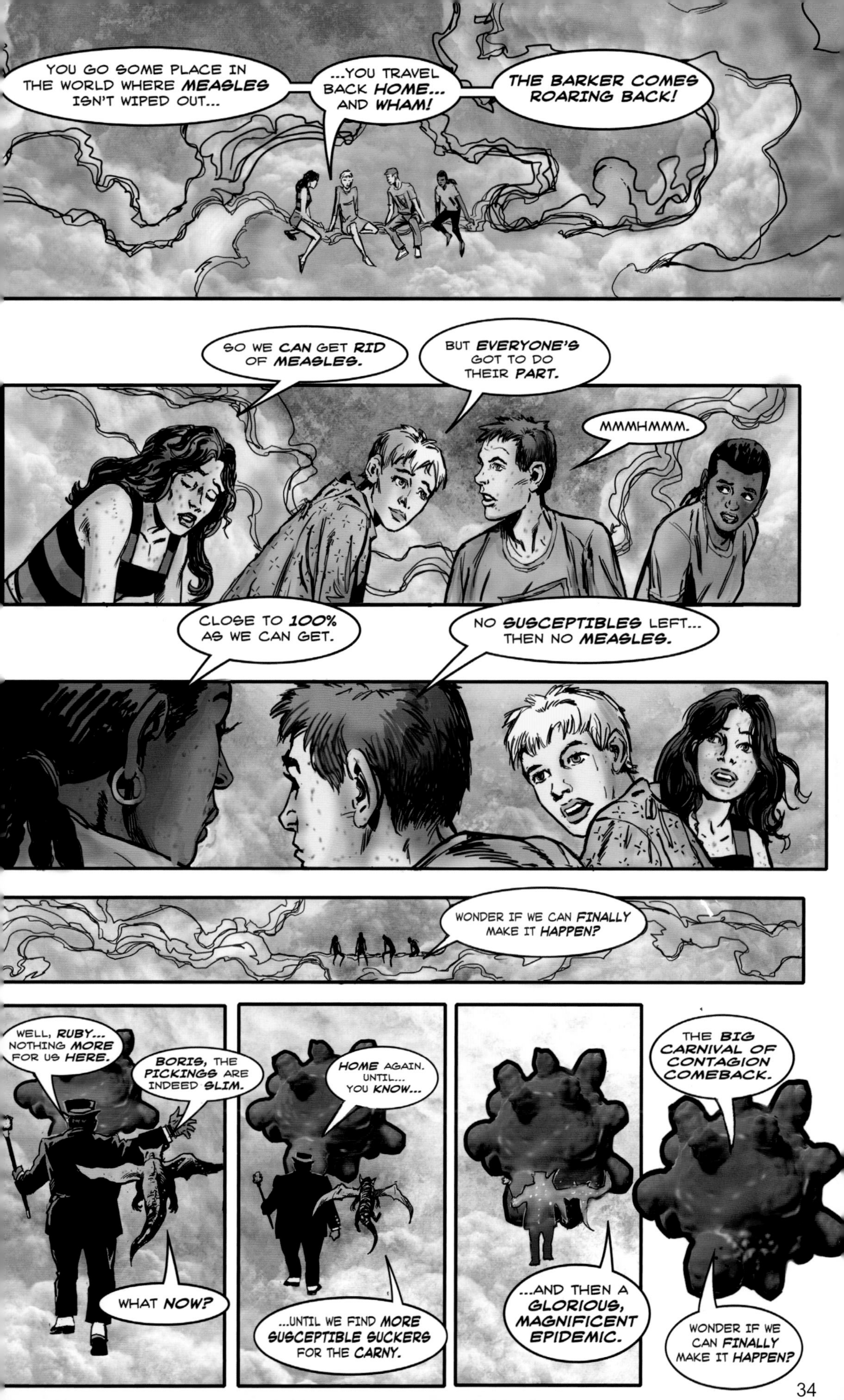
YOU GO SOME PLACE IN THE WORLD WHERE MEASLES ISN'T WIPED OUT...
...YOU TRAVEL BACK HOME... AND WHAM!
THE BARKER COMES ROARING BACK!
SO WE CAN GET RID OF MEASLES.
BUT EVERYONE'S GOT TO DO THEIR PART.
MMMHMMM.
CLOSE TO 100% AS WE CAN GET.
NO SUSCEPTIBLES LEFT... THEN NO MEASLES.
WONDER IF WE CAN FINALLY MAKE IT HAPPEN?
WELL, RUBY... NOTHING MORE FOR US HERE.
BORIS, THE PICKINGS ARE INDEED SLIM.
WHAT NOW?
HOME AGAIN. UNTIL... YOU KNOW...
...UNTIL WE FIND MORE SUSCEPTIBLE SUCKERS FOR THE CARNY.
...AND THEN A GLORIOUS, MAGNIFICENT EPIDEMIC.
THE BIG CARNIVAL OF CONTAGION COMEBACK.
WONDER IF WE CAN FINALLY MAKE IT HAPPEN?

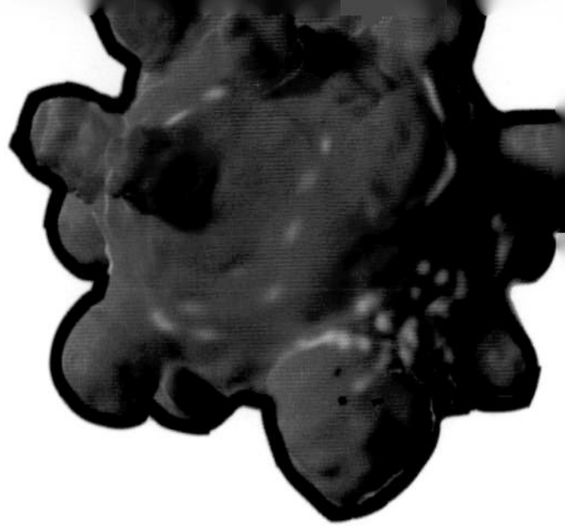

MASTER OF CONTAGION

Carl Zimmer

In 1846 a young Danish doctor named Peter Panum arrived at the Faroe Islands, a windswept archipelago situated between Iceland and Scotland. The Danish government had dispatched Panum on a mission. An outbreak of measles was tormenting the islands and Panum was to report back to Copenhagen on the situation.

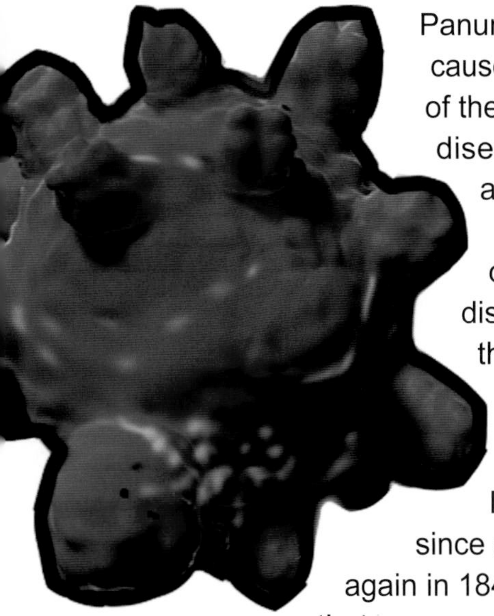

Panum, of course, had no idea that the outbreak was caused by a virus. In 1846 no one could even conceive of the idea. The very concept of viruses as agents of disease would not emerge for another fifty years, and the measles virus itself wouldn't be discovered until 1954. In Panum's day, doctors could merely catalogue the symptoms of the measles—the distinctive red blotches that spread across the body, the fevers, the slow recovery.

How people became sick with measles was a mystery. Before Panum's journey to the Faroe Islands, no one there had suffered from measles since an outbreak in 1781. Why the disease flared up again in 1846 was anyone's guess. Many doctors believed that new measles outbreaks occurred when an invisible, disease-causing substance called miasma rose from the ground and drifted through the air, sickening everyone in its path. They had no evidence for the actual existence of miasma, just the vague sense that diseases had a way of enveloping communities like a fog.

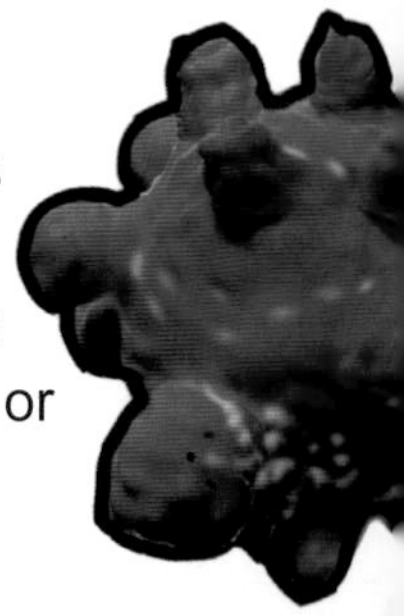

During his time on the islands, Panum carefully recorded the details of his visits to a thousand patients. He wrote vividly about people in the throes of the disease: "The patients were bathed in perspiration," Panum wrote, "and, when the bedding was raised or the shin exposed, vapors literally rose from them like clouds."

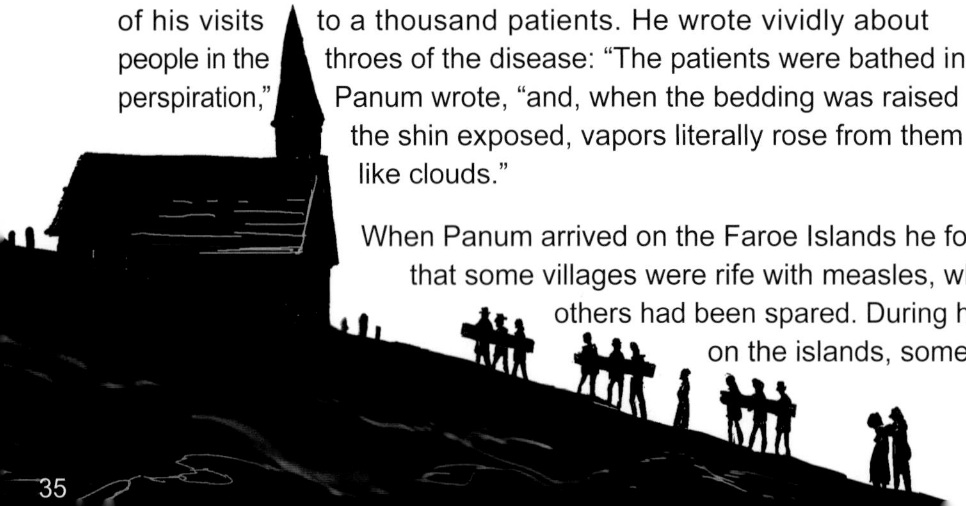

When Panum arrived on the Faroe Islands he found that some villages were rife with measles, while others had been spared. During his stay on the islands, some of the

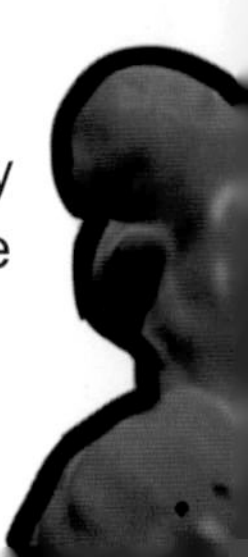

healthy villages fell ill. As the disease spread, he mapped the rise of new cases from village to village and then within villages. Looking at his records, he saw a pattern that didn't match what he would have expected from miasma. The measles did not march across islands, infecting every village in its path. Instead, the disease leaped from an infected village to a healthy one. In some cases, Panum could identify the sick person who carried the disease to its new home.

Panum worked out the timing of the disease. If one person developed a rash from measles, Panum knew that other people living in that person's house would get sick two weeks later. He also studied the path that the disease took from person to person. On average, he estimated, every infected Faroese infected seven to nine others.

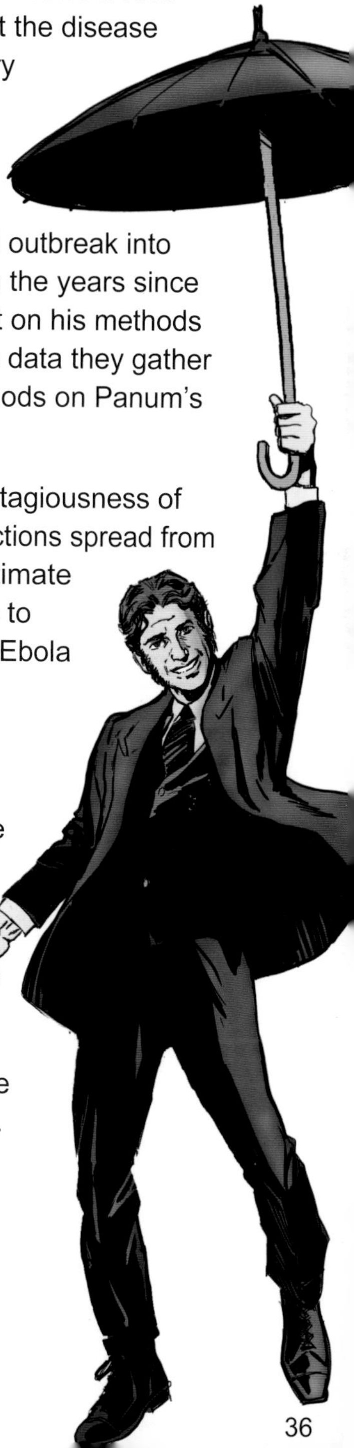

The report Panum wrote for the Danish government stands today as a landmark in the history of medicine. For the first time someone had distilled the chaos and suffering of a viral outbreak into the remarkably mathematical regularities of epidemiology. In the years since Panum's trip to the Faroe Islands, epidemiologists have built on his methods developing better ways to survey populations and to use the data they gather to build a profile of a pathogen. But they built their new methods on Panum's strong foundations.

Remarkably, it turns out that Panum underestimated the contagiousness of measles. The current estimate for the average number of infections spread from each sick person is between twelve and eighteen. That estimate puts measles at the top of the list of viruses when it comes to contagiousness. (By comparison, each person infected with Ebola infects only about two other people on average.)

The extraordinary contagiousness of the measles emerges from its strategy for replicating. Like any virus, the measles virus has to do three things in order to avoid extinction: invade a new host, make copies of itself, and get those copies to another host. At every step of the way, scientists are finding, the measles virus cranks up its chances of a successful spread.

People get infected with measles viruses by breathing them into their lungs. The lining of the lungs contains immune cells that destroy incoming invaders and kill off infected cells. The measles virus boldly attacks these very sentinels. It uses a molecular key to open a passage into the immune cells. Once inside, it starts making new viruses that infect other immune cells.

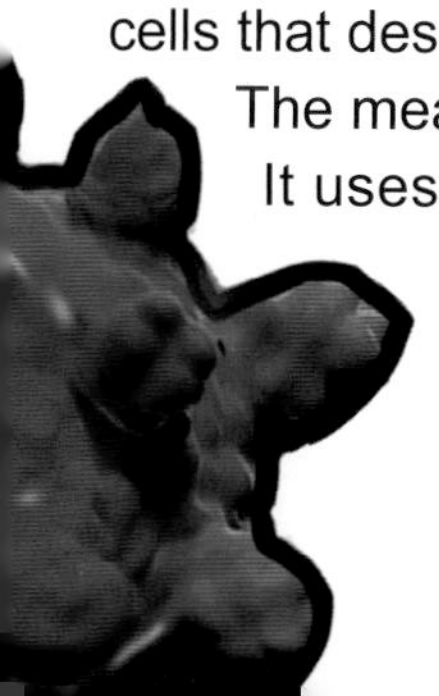

The virus-laden cells then creep from the windpipe to the lymph nodes, which are crowded with still more immune cells. From the lymph nodes, infected immune cells spread the virus throughout the body. If the virus manages to slip into the nervous system it can cause permanent brain damage.

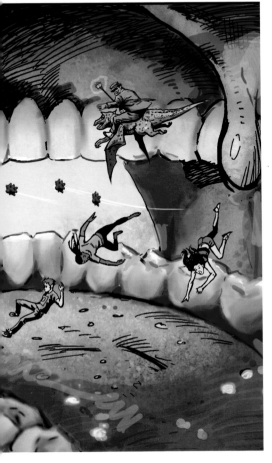

After several days of multiplying, the virus enters a new phase of existence in which it makes preparations to leave its host. Some of the infected immune cells creep up into their host's nose and nuzzle up to the cells that make up the lining of the nose, called epithelial cells. The measles virus carries a protein that can fuse its immune cell to an epithelial cell and open a passage.

Each infected epithelial cell in the nose starts making huge numbers of new measles viruses. The nose becomes clogged with mucus, which is loaded with the new viruses. With each exhalation some of those viruses can escape the nose and float into the air. At the same time, the damage to the upper airway from the infection causes infected cells to rip free and get coughed out of the body.

People sick with measles can thus release clouds of virus-laden droplets. The big droplets fall quickly to the ground or other surfaces, where they can stay infectious for hours. The small droplets meanwhile rise into the air, where they are lofted by currents and can deliver measles to people far away.

The sheer number of viruses produced by each sick person, along with the adaptations the viruses have for penetrating deep into the airway, make them tremendously contagious. If someone gets sick with measles, up to 90 percent of people in the same home who aren't already immune will get sick too. And because infected people can transmit the virus for days before symptoms emerge, the virus can spread to many homes before anyone realizes an outbreak is underway.

The late-arriving symptoms of measles are the outward sign that people's immune systems are starting to fight the virus. Much of the battle takes place between uninfected immune cells and infected ones. Once the civil war is over, the immune system is left decimated and weak. It can take weeks after a measles infection for people's immune system to get back to full strength.

In this fragile state, victims of measles can become vulnerable to other diseases such as pneumonia. The danger posed by these infections depends on how much care patients can get. In industrialized countries, only a tenth of 1 percent of people who get measles die. In developing countries the rate is 5 to 10 percent. In refugee camps the figure can be as high as 25 percent.

While people are coping with these postinfection troubles, the virus has moved on to its next hosts. The contagion of measles is part of a "one-and-done" strategy that the viruses have evolved. After people recover from measles infections, their immune systems will protect them for life. As a result, the virus needs to be highly contagious for its long-term survival.

This strategy also means that measles vaccines can be extremely effective. By teaching people's immune systems what the measles virus looks like, vaccines provide protection for life.

All these features of the measles virus add up to a startling paradox. Despite being far more contagious than the Ebola virus, the measles virus is a far better candidate for complete eradication from the face of the Earth.

Ebola viruses mainly circulate between animals (scientists suspect bats are their normal host). Every few years they get into humans and cause an outbreak. Bringing Ebola outbreaks to a halt doesn't mean that the virus has become extinct. It just means that it has retreated back to its regular host.

Measles, on the other hand, infects only humans. If we could make our species measles-free, that would mean the virus had become extinct, never to return. And the life cycle of measles actually makes it possible to block its transmission from person to person. It's very rare for infections to last more than a couple weeks, so that there

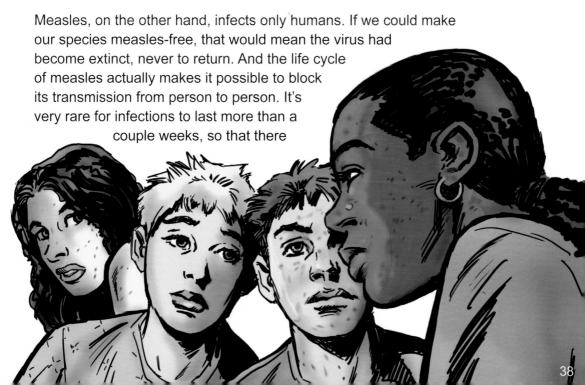

isn't the risk of people surreptitiously spreading the disease for years. People who do get sick won't get sick again, taking them out of the pool of potential hosts. And we are fortunate to have a safe, effective way to break measles transmission: a vaccine.

Before the development of measles vaccines in the early 1960s, 7 to 8 million children died around the world every year. In 2014 that figure was down to 145,000 deaths. The World Health Organization estimates that between 2000 and 2013, measles vaccination prevented 15.6 million deaths. In the coming decade, new vaccination campaigns now being launched may drive down deaths from measles even more.

These victories have been hard won, and they can be easily reversed. In order to use a vaccine to wipe out a virus from a country, it's necessary to immunize most people. That strategy makes it difficult for viruses to spread from one person to another. When new viruses emerge from a host, they're likely to encounter people with strong immune defenses rather than vulnerable victims. If the virus can't sustain its numbers by infecting new hosts, it will sputter out completely.

This collective protection is known as herd immunity. And the percentage of a population that must be vaccinated to achieve herd immunity varies from virus to virus. Because measles is so contagious, 95 percent of a population has to be vaccinated against it to achieve herd immunity. Anything less will allow the virus to find enough vulnerable hosts to sustain its population.

To eradicate the measles from a country, a single vaccination campaign is not enough. Children need to be vaccinated to avoid creating a vulnerable population that can rear the virus. By 2000, for example, the United States had reduced measles to the point that it could no longer circulate on its own inside the country. Infected people from other countries sometimes managed to spread measles to a few Americans each year, but the high level of vaccination helped keep those outbreaks low. But since then, vaccination rates have slipped in some communities. Parents have gotten their children exempted from measles vaccination, often because of religious objections or because they have unfounded worries that the vaccine causes autism (a claim that has been thoroughly refuted). As a result, in recent years the United States has seen much bigger outbreaks of the measles. In December 2014 someone infected with measles visited Disneyland and infected a number of other people at the park. By April the outbreak had spread to seven states and infected 147 people.

It's possible that these recent outbreaks will mark a turning point—a recognition that vaccination is a social contract we make to each other so that we don't allow the virus to infect our fellow citizens. Perhaps we will someday even eradicate measles completely. That will unquestionably be a boon for humanity. But it's also possible that it could open the way to a new disease. That's because the measles virus has cousins.

Measles belongs to a cluster of viruses called morbilliviruses. They infect a wide range of animals, from whales to wildebeest, from pandas to primates. It appears that morbilliviruses use the same strategy as measles—coming in through immune cells and going out through epithelial cells. And they're also just as contagious. Some studies suggest that measles started out several thousand years ago as one of these wild morbilliviruses. According to one theory, after we domesticated cattle, a cow morbillivirus jumped into humans. As human populations grew dense, the new measles viruses found a comfortable new home.

Scientists have documented virtually no cases of morbilliviruses spreading from animals to humans. Given the staggering contagiousness of morbilliviruses, that's pretty remarkable. It's possible that our immunity to measles also protects us from other morbilliviruses. These animal viruses may sometimes make incursions into our species, but the conditions are so harsh that they never have time to adapt to our biology. If that's true, eradicating measles might open up a new ecological niche that another animal morbillivirus could take over.

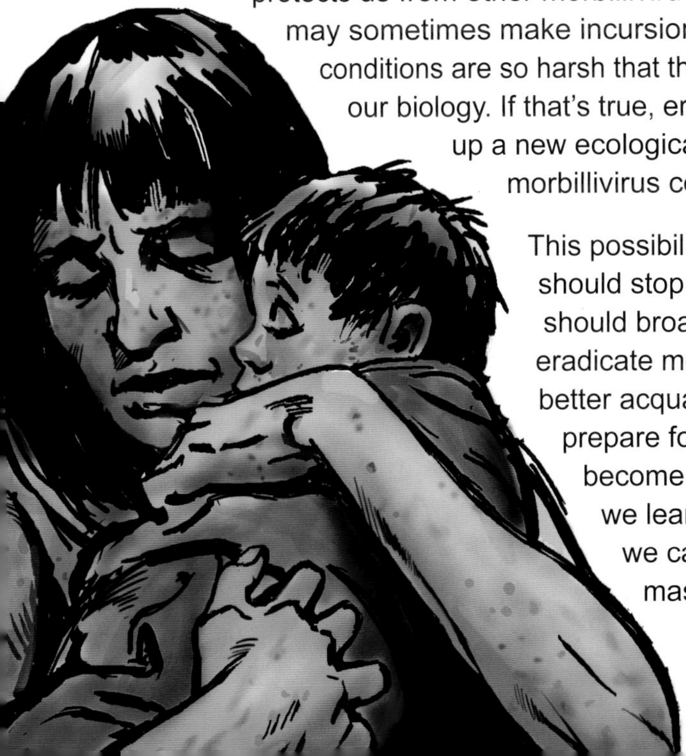

This possibility doesn't mean that we should stop fighting measles. Instead, we should broaden our efforts. Even as we eradicate measles, we should become better acquainted with related viruses and prepare for the possibility that they may become new threats. With the lessons we learn from eradicating measles, we can be ready to battle the next master of contagion.

The Biology of Human project was funded by the National Institutes of Health (NIH) through the Science Education Partnership Award (SEPA) Grant No. 1R25OD010506. Its content is solely the responsibility of the authors and does not necessarily represent the official views of the NIH. Principal investigators are Judy Diamond, University of Nebraska State Museum; Julia McQuillan, Department of Sociology at the University of Nebraska–Lincoln; and Charles Wood, Nebraska Center for Virology.

Many scientists and educators guided our work and reviewed its production. We especially acknowledge the help of Bridget Agnew, Linda Allison, Abby Heithoff, Patricia Wonch Hill, Troy Mack, La'Risa McLennon, Rebecca Smith, Amy Spiegel, Sara LeRoy-Toren, Camillia Matuk, Adam Wagler, Ilonka Zlatar, students in the Culler Middle School afterschool program, and our NIH-SEPA program officer, Tony Beck.

For information see http://biologyofhuman.unl.edu.

SEPA SCIENCE EDUCATION PARTNERSHIP AWARD
Supported by the National Center for Research Resources, a part of the National Institutes of Health

UNIVERSITY OF NEBRASKA STATE MUSEUM

UNIVERSITY OF Nebraska Lincoln